Starting
Your Career
as a
Marine Mammal
Trainer

by

Terry S. Samansky

Starting Your Career as a Marine Mammal Trainer

Publisher's Cataloging-in-Publication
(Provided by Quality Books, Inc.)

Samansky, Terry S.
    Starting your career as a marine mammal trainer / by Terry S. Samansky. -- 2nd ed.
        p. cm.
    Includes bibliographical references and index.
    LCCN: 2002091471
    ISBN: 0971985324

    1. Marine mammals--Training. 2. Animal training--Vocational guidance.   I. Title.

SF408.6.M37S36 2002   636.95'023
                             QBIO2-200320

Published by
DolphinTrainer.com
1370 Trancas Street #402
Napa, CA 94558 USA
                http://www.dolphintrainer.com

Table of Contents

*This book is dedicated to
the men and women who devote their lives
to care for, train, study and protect
dolphins, whales, seals, sea lions, walruses
and other marine mammals.*

The pathway is made clearer when we follow in the footsteps of pioneers with vision and courage. Pioneer, mentor and friend Sonny Allen doing what he loved best.

ACKNOWLEDGMENTS

The production of this book could not have been possible without the valuable contributions of several fine and talented people. Special thanks to Madelyn Parker, Michelle Mecchi, Sue Negrini, Kerri McDowell, Jeff Jouett and Sudie White.

We are all influenced and shaped by the people in our lives. Luckily, I have been blessed with a wonderful family, supportive friends and generous colleagues. I would love to personally thank each and every one of you by name, but the sheer volume (and my desire not to inadvertently exclude anyone) makes that task impossible.

Because the focus of this book is career development, I would be remiss if I did not acknowledge five marine mammal specialists who have contributed so much to my own professional growth. Thank you to Brad, Jay, Scott, Tim and Sonny. You have all been my supervisors, mentors, role models and friends. I cannot count the number of times that I have looked for the resolution of a problem or approached a challenge by first asking myself the question, "What would you guys do in a situation such as this?"

Finally, thanks to Six Flags Marine World for many years of support, opportunity and experience and for many of the fine photographs presented throughout this book.

During a night show at Six Flags Marine World, killer whale Vigga leaps over a trainer (in this case the author), demonstrating the power and grace of this incredible creature, as well as the trust and respect that must exist between the trainer and the animal.

INTRODUCTION

How did you get such a cool job?

Like most people I know who are fortunate enough to actually work with marine mammals, I hear this question a lot. Young people especially want to know how I and other animal professionals got started in this field and, more importantly, how they can too. This career guide is dedicated to helping people learn what it's really like to be a marine mammal trainer and what steps they can take to enter and succeed in this profession.

My fascination with these intriguing animals began at a very early age. In fact, I really can't remember a time when I didn't dream of becoming a dolphin trainer. I always knew that I wanted to work with these seemingly mysterious creatures and really get to know them on a personal basis. For over twenty years now, I have been living that dream, working side by side with dolphins, whales, seals, sea lions and walruses.

As a child, my favorite TV shows were nature programs like National Geographic and Jacques Cousteau specials. I spent a lot of time at the local library and read all the books I could find that had anything to do with marine mammals. (I have since learned that a lot of the popular material written in the 1960's and 70's about dolphin intelligence and behavior was either exaggerated or just plain wrong.)

Serious career preparations began in high school and college. Since I wasn't sure what courses a marine mammal trainer needed, I felt a safe bet would be to focus on science, math and English. After a lot of hard work and study, I eventually received my bachelor of arts degree from California State University, Sacramento in biological science with a minor in chemistry. Many people mistakenly think a degree in marine biology or oceanography is required to work with marine mammals. Most people I know who care for and train these animals in zoos and oceanariums have degrees in broader subjects, such as biology, zoology and psychology. These subjects also provide a great foundation for those wishing to go on, get their advanced degrees and conduct research, or become veterinarians.

Getting good grades and a degree was certainly very important, but I also knew I had to acquire some practical experience working with large or exotic animals if I wanted to reach my goal. While still in college, I sent out resumes and applications to every zoo and oceanarium I could think of. I was hoping to get a summer job working with exotic animals, preferably marine mammals, while still an undergraduate. I knew that this kind of experience would be invaluable when I finally graduated and began applying for my first regular full-time marine mammal position.

After two years of applying for numerous animal positions, my big break came in the summer between my junior and senior years when I was offered a seasonal keeper position at Marineland in Palos Verdes, California. All the hard work, preparation and determination finally began to pay off that first summer. Marineland provided me with my first practical hands-on experience with real live marine mammals. I was able to meet and learn from people who were doing exactly what I wanted to do. And, it allowed me to experience firsthand what it was really like to be a marine mammal professional.

That summer turned out to be a significant turning point in my career and my life. From my first day on the job, I knew this was the right vocational choice for me. The animals were great, of course, but I discovered something else that summer that I hadn't counted on; something that has kept me active in this field for over two decades. I found that I deeply respect and love working with people who devote their lives to care for, train and study these animals.

People who do this kind of work don't make much money. It's often hard physical labor. Trainers are frequently in the water and/or wet much of the time. They work in all kinds of weather, on holidays and weekends and are often on call for unexpected events. Trainers generally spend more time with their animals than they do their own families. They care deeply for their animals and suffer when one of them gets sick or passes away.

Trainers share a common passion and devotion to the animals that exists beyond the borders of any individual facility, institution or country. This universal connection is one of the reasons I enjoy attending professional conferences and visiting other marine mammal facilities. Wherever I go, at home or abroad, I am inspired, re-energized and filled with pride by the dedication and true camaraderie that exists in the international marine mammal display, research and educational community. I've often said that I got into this field for the animals, but I stay in it for the people.

Ever since that first summer, one of my primary goals has been to grow and advance as a productive member of this community. Over the years, I have held positions as a marine mammal keeper, rehabilitation specialist, trainer, curator, director and consultant at facilities in the United States, Japan and South America. In addition to Marineland, which closed in 1987, I have worked for companies such as Marine World Africa USA, Active Environments and Six Flags Marine World.

In all that time I've never lost my initial fascination for these unique and engaging creatures, and my respect and commitment to protect them has only increased. Through continued study, personal experience and observation I have learned quite a bit about these animals and the vital role they play as integral parts of the earth's marine ecosystems. I've tried to share this knowledge and personal insight with others through published articles, papers and book chapters, multimedia presentations, college classes, Web sites and now this career guide.

Like anyone who has worked with marine mammals for many years, I have been asked countless questions about the animals and my profession. While many of the questions are about the animals' natural history, care and training, the majority of questions I get are from young people who want to know more about this field as a possible career choice. Many people today are still fascinated by the idea of working side by side with these unique animals, developing strong personal relationships with them and helping them to grow, develop and stay healthy, strong and protected. It is my hope that this career guide will help answer most of these questions and offer some valuable insights to anyone interested in this profession as a possible career choice.

To get the most out of *Starting Your Career as a Marine Mammal Trainer,* you are encouraged to read each chapter in sequence, including the introductory pages of each resource section. If you do this, you may notice that a couple of important themes are repeated several times. This is to ensure that those readers who choose to skip around or use this document solely as reference source do not miss critical information.

As you explore this book, remember, it can only be a guide. There are few hard and fast rules, and no sure things. There are many roads to becoming a marine mammal professional, but only you can choose the best path for you.

A trainer's primary responsibility is to maintain and enhance the health and well-being of the animals in their care. Fortunately, that can be one of the most enjoyable and rewarding parts of the job, as well. In this photo, trainers from Six Flags Marine World bottle feed two orphaned Pacific walrus calves. These animals adapt well to their new environment and thrive in human care.

Like all present-day marine mammals, dolphins are superbly adapted to life in an aquatic environment and display all five definitive mammalian characteristics. In this photo, a bottlenose dolphin leaps out of the water and into a powerful forward flip, gracefully symbolizing the ties to both water and air shared by all marine mammals.

THE ANIMALS

B efore you can explore the career of a marine mammal trainer, you need to understand a little bit about the basic nature of the animals they work with. This chapter will begin by reviewing the five essential characteristics required for an animal to be classified as a mammal. Next, a broad overview of the group of animals collectively called marine mammals will be presented. This will be followed by more specific information about one particular species of marine mammal, the bottlenose dolphin.

EXPLORING MARINE MAMMALS

The following information will answer some of the basic questions that marine mammal trainers are asked about the natural history and biology of their animals.

What is a mammal?

Mammals are vertebrate animals (animals with backbones or spinal columns) that also possess all five of the following characteristics:

1) They have lungs and breathe air.
2) They are warm-blooded and maintain a constant body temperature.
3) Most bear live young. One primitive mammal group, the monotremes (which includes the platypus), lays eggs.
4) They produce milk from mammary glands and nurse their young.
5) They have hair (at least at some point in their lives.)

You can probably think of many examples of animals that live on land and meet the five basic characteristics required to be a classified as a mammal. Some of these animals include dogs, horses, cats, rats, pigs and people.

What is a marine mammal?

In the most basic terms, marine mammals are mammals that live in a saltwater or (in some cases) a brackish or freshwater environment, and derive most or all of their nutrition from that environment. Most marine mammals live in ocean environments but some, such as freshwater dolphins and some species of seals, may live in rivers and lakes.

Not all mammals that live in the water are considered true marine mammals. River otters and beavers, for example, are mammals that spend a great deal of their lives in water but are not regarded as marine mammals. A table outlining all of the living animal groups that are classified as true marine mammals is presented on page 19.

It's easy to see why seals, sea lions, walruses, sea otters and polar bears are classified as marine mammals. They live in aquatic environments and certainly meet all five of the classic mammalian criteria. But what about dolphins, whales and porpoises? They are classified as marine mammals, but do they have hair? Yes, very early in life even these sleek, smooth animals possess a small amount of hair. It can be seen around their mouths and is usually lost soon after birth. If you have the opportunity to look closely at an adult cetacean (whale, dolphin or porpoise) you can still see the raised follicles where the hair used to be. Hair in cetaceans no longer serves a useful function. It is considered a vestigial trait carried over from their land dwelling ancestors.

All marine mammals were originally land mammals, and share common ancestry and characteristics with every other mammal. Over time, the ancestors of modern marine mammals became increasingly specialized to meet the challenges of life in an aquatic environment. For example, cetaceans (animals that live their entire lives in the water) have little need for hair. In fact, hair can be a problem by acting as a drag to slow these animals down as they speed through the water. To be more hydrodynamic and efficient in the water, cetaceans have lost almost all of their hair. On the other hand, slower swimming marine mammals that still spend a lot of their time on land, such as polar bears and sea otters, still rely heavily on the protection and insulation that their hair or fur provides.

What are the four orders of marine mammals?

Scientists classify all types of organisms by their genetic relationships to each other. This process is called taxonomy. As you have already seen, to be classified as a mammal one must possess all five characteristics listed on page 15.

All mammals belong to the class Mammalia. Within this class are 19 living subgroups called orders. Three of these orders are made up entirely of marine mammals. These three orders are Cetacea, Pinnipedia* and Sirenia. A fourth order, Carnivora, contains both marine and land mammals.

* Some scientists believe that the pinniped group should be classified as a suborder of Carnivora. This book will agree with those scientists and authors that classify Pinnipedia as its own separate order.

The four orders of present day marine mammals:

Cetaceans –	made up entirely of whales, dolphins and porpoises
Pinnipeds –	made up entirely of seals, sea lions and walruses
Sirenians –	made up entirely of dugongs and manatees
Carnivores –	includes sea otters and polar bears (also includes other nonmarine mammals such as dogs, cats and foxes.)

A highly social species, five young Atlantic bottlenose dolphins, all born at Six Flags Marine World, seek out and enjoy interacting with each other, their trainers and park guests (in this case through an underwater viewing window).

Table 1 - Taxonomic Classification of Living Marine Mammals

Classification	Scientific Name	Common Name
Kingdom	Animalia	Animals
Phylum	Chordata	Animals w/ notochords
Subphylum	Vertebrata	Vertebrates
Class	Mammalia	Mammals
Order	Cetacea	Cetaceans
Suborder	Odontoceti	Toothed Cetaceans
Family	Physeteridae	Sperm Whales
Family	Ziphiidae	Beaked & Bottlenosed Whales
Family	Delphinidae	Marine Dolphins
Family	Platanistidae	Freshwater Dolphins
Family	Phocoenidae	Porpoises
Family	Monodontidae	Belugas & Narwhals
Suborder	Mysticeti	Baleen Whales
Family	Balaenopteridae	Rorquals
Family	Balaenidae	Right Whales
Family	Eschrichtiidae	Gray Whales
Order	Sirenia	Dugongs & Manatees
Family	Dugongidae	Dugongs
Family	Trichechidae	Manatees
Order	Pinnipedia	Pinnipeds
Family	Phocidae	True or Earless Seals
Family	Otariidae	Sea Lions or Eared Seals
Family	Odobenidae	Walruses
Order	Carnivora	Carnivores
Family	Mustelidae	Sea Otters
Family	Ursidae	Polar Bears

This table provides a complete taxonomic chart of all known living (nonextinct) marine mammal families.

SPECIES PROFILE: BOTTLENOSE DOLPHINS
(*Tursiops truncatus*)

While it is not practical to thoroughly review every marine mammal species in a book of this nature, the rest of this chapter will examine one very popular and well-known species within the marine mammal group, the bottlenose dolphin.

The "Classic" Dolphin

When most people think of a dolphin, the bottlenose dolphin (*Tursiops truncatus*) is the species that comes to mind. It may surprise some people to learn that scientists have actually classified over 35 different species of marine and freshwater dolphins. These different dolphin species display a wide variety of body shapes, sizes and color patterns, however, the classic gray bottlenose dolphin is certainly the one most widely recognized. Not only is this the species most often found in zoological parks and aquariums, but it is also the one usually featured in popular books, television programs and movies, such as *Flipper*.

Much of what we know about cetacean physiology, reproduction, nutritional requirements, medical care, behavior, cognition, learning and echolocation has been derived from observing and working with bottlenose dolphins in modern marine parks and aquariums. Members of this species adapt and do well in these controlled environments. They live long, healthy lives and reproduce well. They are naturally curious, playful animals and form strong bonds with their human caregivers.

Scientific Classification

Order: .....Cetacea (whales, dolphins and porpoises)
   Suborder: ....Odontoceti (toothed cetaceans)
     Family: ....Delphinidae (marine dolphins)
       Genus: ....*Tursiops*
         Species: ....*T. truncatus*

Although most scientists today recognize just one species of bottlenose dolphin (*Tursiops truncatus*), they usually describe at least three subspecies or races. These include the Atlantic bottlenose dolphin (*T. truncatus*), the Pacific bottlenose dolphin (*T. truncatus gilli*) and the Southern Hemisphere bottlenose dolphin (*T. truncatus aduncus*). Some physical characteristics vary so much between these groups that some scientists suggest they be classified as completely separate species. This book will agree with most authors and consider all bottlenose dolphins to be members of a single species, *Tursiops truncatus*.

Illustration 1 - Bottlenose Dolphin External Anatomy

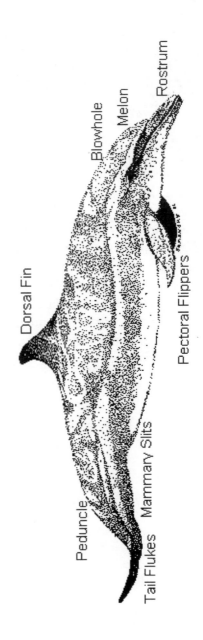

Physical Description

General body shape:
The dolphin body is torpedo shaped to provide a hydrodynamic profile and reduced resistance as the animal glides through the water. (See *Illustration 1* on page 22.) The upper jaw of cetaceans is often referred to as the rostrum. In this species the rostrum and lower jaw extend out several inches past the large forehead (or melon area) and serve as the basis for its common name, bottlenose dolphin. In reality, the nose is nowhere near this area. As with all cetaceans, the nose is actually located on top of the head and is called the blowhole. With the nasal opening positioned on top of the head, the dolphin is able to rapidly exhale and inhale without having to lift its entire head above the surface of the water. In this respect, the blowhole functions in the same way as a skin diver's snorkel.

Midway down the back is a prominent sickle-shaped dorsal fin that provides stabilization (something like the keel of a sailboat.) Just behind the head area are two medium sized pectoral flippers that help with steering and direction (similar in function to the forward planes on a submarine.) The vast majority of the dolphin's propulsion comes from its powerful tail flukes. The flukes are located at the end of the extremely muscular tail stock, or peduncle.

It may be interesting to note that the tail flukes of all cetaceans lie in a horizontal plane and propel the animal forward by moving up and down. The tail fins of fish, on the other hand, lie in a vertical plane and propel these animals forward by moving side to side.

Color:
The primary color of the bottlenose dolphin varies from very dark to light gray. This color is darker on the top, or dorsal, surface of the animal. It gradually lightens as it moves down to the belly, or ventral, region. The ventral surface of the animal may be pure white, although at times it may also show hues ranging from pink to yellow.

This coloration pattern of dark on top and light on the bottom is a classic example of countershading, which is common in many cetacean species. It is thought that this color system helps camouflage the animal, making it less visible to both predators and prey alike. When viewed from above, the dark dorsal surface of the dolphin blends in with the dark water and sea floor below. When viewed from below, the light underside blends in with the bright sky and shimmering surface of the water above.

Size:
Depending upon the subspecies, adults may attain lengths of up to 13 feet (4 meters) and weights of 1,450 lbs (658 kg). The most common subspecies found in US oceanariums, the Atlantic bottlenose dolphin, is generally a much smaller animal. Adult Atlantic bottlenose dolphins range in length from 6 – 9 feet (1.8 – 2.7 m) and attain weights ranging from 300 – 500 lbs (136 - 227 kg). At birth, calves are usually 35 – 50 inches (89 – 127 cm) in length and may weigh from 30 – 90 lbs (14 – 41 kg).

Natural History and Reproduction

Distribution:
Bottlenose dolphins are found in temperate and tropical waters around the world.

Diet:
The primary diet of this species is small fish, which are caught and usually swallowed whole. Depending upon the availability of prey species, bottlenose dolphins may also eat larger fish, squid, octopus, crabs and shrimp. Large food items may be torn into pieces to make swallowing easier. Larger subspecies, such as the Pacific bottlenose dolphin, may eat up to 35 lbs (16 kg) per day. Pregnant or nursing females may consume even more.

Maximum swimming speed:
Approximately 20 miles per hour (32 kph).

Echolocation:
Like all odontocetes, dolphins can locate and identify objects by emitting sounds and listening to their reflected echos.

Sexual maturity:
Males: 7 – 12 years of age.
Females: 5 – 10 years of age.

Gestation period:
Approximately 12 months.

Calf size:
Length: 35 – 50 inches (89 – 127 cm).
Weight: 30 – 90 lbs (13.6 – 41 kg).

Number of calves:
Normally one calf per pregnancy. While twin fetuses have been reported, this is thought to be very rare and none are known to have survived.

Calving period:
Usually spring and summer.

Nursing process:
Female dolphins possess two mammary glands that produce a rich milk to nourish their young. The calf feeds on this milk by placing the tip of its rostrum against one of the two mammary slits located on the ventral surface of the mother's body (See *Illustration 1* on page 22.) It then cups its tongue around the nipple that lies within the mammary slit. A tight seal is formed between the calf's tongue and the mother's nipple that allows suckling to take place. The mother can physically eject milk into the calf's mouth to help speed the nursing process. This is very helpful since the whole process takes place under water while both animals hold their breath.

Nursing period:
Young calves may begin eating fish within a few months after birth, but may continue to nurse for one to two years or more.

Calving interval:
Approximately every two to four years.

Calf survival rate:
Approximately 40–50% of all calves do not survive their first year of life. Maternal bond and experience are extremely important to calf survival in a challenging aquatic environment, and both factors increase with the mother's age and each successive pregnancy. Consequently, infant survival is much lower with very young or inexperienced mothers.

This has been a very brief introduction to the study of marine mammals. Anyone wishing to work with these animals will certainly need a much more detailed understanding of these fascinating creatures. For a few recommended books on this subject see the Suggested Readings section, starting on page 132.

THE CAREER

Now that you know a little more about the group of animals known as marine mammals, it's time to take a look at the job of caring for and training them.

THE JOB OF A MARINE MAMMAL TRAINER

Ever wonder what it's really like to be a dolphin, whale or sea lion trainer? This section will answer some of the most common questions trainers are asked about their jobs.

What is a marine mammal trainer?

Depending upon the particular facility and its specific operations, the people who care for and train marine mammals in oceanariums, aquariums, marine parks and similar zoological institutions may be called trainers, animal care specialists, keepers, naturalists, mammalogists or various other titles. Most of these professionals start out as assistants or apprentices. After years of hard work and progress, they may earn new titles denoting higher levels of achievement and authority, such as seniors, leads, supervisors, managers, curators or directors. For the sake of simplicity, we will just refer to all of these hands-on marine mammal professionals as trainers.

Is a marine mammal trainer the same thing as a marine biologist?

Trainers often hear people say, "I want to be a marine biologist and train dolphins." While it is true that some marine biologists do train dolphins, and many trainers have degrees in biology, the two job descriptions are really quite different.

Many individuals mistakenly lump marine mammal trainers, marine biologists and oceanographers into one homogenous group. Oceanographers primarily study the physical aspects of the world's oceans. This includes their chemical, geologic and atmospheric natures. A marine biologist is someone who studies life in the seas and oceans. They may specialize in such areas as physiology, behavior or ecology. The subjects of their investigations may range from microscopic single-celled organisms to 150-ton blue whales.

Proportionately, very few marine biologists and oceanographers work hands-on with or train living marine mammals. A good marine mammal trainer may study and use knowledge from both of these fields (and more), but each of these careers is really part of its own specialized discipline.

What does a marine mammal trainer actually do?

A trainer's primary responsibility is to maintain and enhance the health and well-being of the animals in their care. To achieve this vital goal, trainers must understand and work hard to ensure that their animals are provided with the highest quality food, aquatic environments, structural habitats, social and behavioral opportunities and medical care.

To survive in an aquatic environment, marine mammals have become highly specialized creatures. Their anatomy, physiology and behavior have adapted to meet the challenges of life in the sea. Consequently, to care for them properly in zoos, oceanariums and aquariums, the facilities, operating systems and staff must be highly specialized as well.

Like other zoo animals, marine mammals need to be provided such things as well-designed and maintained living spaces, proper food, physical and mental stimulation and compatible social groupings. In addition, marine mammal habitats must include larger bodies of water designed to accommodate the individual needs of each species. All marine mammal species require the quality of their pool water to be maintained at very high standards. Facilities located near oceans or other bodies of unpolluted sea water may circulate and utilize water directly from this natural source. In some cases animals may be housed in netted-off sea pens, built directly within these salt water locations. Facilities that do not have access to naturally occurring sources of clean sea water must design elaborate systems to pump, filter, disinfect and regulate the temperature of artificially made sea water. These specialized systems are so important to the health and well-being of marine mammals that many facilities refer to them as the Life Support Systems (LSS).

Training can be an extremely powerful tool in helping to meet critical animal needs. For example, animals are routinely taught husbandry or veterinary behaviors that allow the staff to monitor and track their health status, and even treat them when necessary with the least amount of delay or stress. Some of these incredibly useful behaviors include the voluntary collection of blood, gastric, urine and fecal samples; physical, X-ray, ultrasonic and dental examinations; and the administration of medicines, replacement fluids and even physical therapy.

Without training, these types of veterinary procedures usually require a much greater degree of planning, staff participation and physical restraint. Through advanced methods of training, marine mammals can now be taught to voluntarily participate in these behaviors, as often as needed, without restraint or discomfort (to themselves or the staff.)

This ability to more quickly and easily perform critical diagnostic procedures enables the veterinarians to get much more accurate assessments of the animals' health status before they show any obvious outward signs of illness. This is extremely important because marine mammals are notorious for their ability to mask or hide illness. Many scientists believe that this adaptation of appearing healthy and strong, even when very sick or weak, has evolved as an important survival mechanism. In the wild, an animal that appears weak or ill makes an inviting target for a hungry predator, such as a shark or killer whale.

Training also provides a valuable tool for facilitating the movement and relocation of animals from one area to another. A procedure, often called "gating", is just one example of how animals can be taught to assist in their own safe movement and relocation. Gating is one of the first and most important behaviors taught. One example of gating would be training a sea lion to walk from one enclosed holding area to another, and wait while a door or gate is closed behind him. Another example would be teaching a group of dolphins to swim from a show pool to a holding pool on cue, as a gate is closed behind them. Being able to quickly, easily and safely move animals helps to effectively manage the population and maintain the most compatible social groupings.

The value of exercise is well-documented, and many independent researchers now agree with what trainers have known for a long time; training provides very valuable mental and physical stimulation. Training is an important and highly adaptable form of exercise and behavioral enrichment, both of which are important for long-term health and well-being.

As a result of all this training and proactive health management, marine mammals in modern zoological facilities are living much longer and healthier lives than ever before. In fact, many of these animals are outliving their counterparts in the wild.

The same training methods and techniques used to teach the animals to participate in their own husbandry and medical care are utilized to train behaviors to help educate and entertain people through shows, demonstrations and public interactive programs. For many people, a visit to a public zoological facility may be the only opportunity they will ever have to experience first-hand the true quality and beauty of these creatures. The animals that participate in these experiences serve as ambassadors for their species. Over the years they have inspired and moved millions of people to learn more about marine mammals and to actively participate in the protection of these animals (and their critical habitats) in the wild.

How do they train all those different behaviors?

At first, the process of training may seem quite complex and perhaps even a bit mysterious. Some people mistakenly refer to trained behaviors as tricks. But, good training isn't magic, an illusion or a trick. It's really just a form of highly effective learning. It's the trainers' job not only to teach the animals, but to do it in such a way that the animals enjoy participating in the process and benefit from the experience. To be effective teachers, trainers must spend a lot of time with their animals and establish strong bonds of mutual trust.

I often refer to training as an art based on science. The basic theory and techniques used in modern marine mammal training are rooted in the science of psychology and behavior analysis. Marine mammal trainers teach their animals using methods of positive reinforcement, part of a behavioral modification system called operant conditioning. In essence, the theory behind operant conditioning provides that the behavior of an animal (or human) will change depending upon the consequences that follow that behavior. For example, any behavior (or response) will likely increase if it is followed by a reward (or reinforcer). This procedure of increasing desired response by rewarding it, is called positive reinforcement and is the basis of modern marine mammal training. How the individual trainer applies these principles, develops training plans, identifies and uses different cues and reinforcers, interacts with the animals and shapes the final trained behavior is truly an artistic process. It may not take long to learn the basic theories and science of training, but it may take a lifetime to master the art.

Fully answering this one question could easily take up an entire book (or several). Fortunately, there are many good books already available on the subject of animal training. A couple of the best ones are listed in the Suggested Readings section, starting on page 132.

How long does it take to train a behavior?

Depending upon the complexity of the particular behavior, the skill of the trainer and the individual intelligence and motivation of the animal, a single trained behavior may take anywhere from one training session to over a year to complete. Trainers, however, do not generally work on just one or two behaviors at a time. They usually work on several different behaviors within each training session. During the course of a day, trainers may work on dozens of different behaviors with each of their animals. Each behavior is completed at its own pace, and previously learned behaviors are practiced often, to maintain quality and consistency. Working on a variety of different behaviors within each training session also helps to maintain interest and enjoyment for both the animals and their trainers.

Are dolphins, sea lions and other marine mammals all trained the same way?

For the most part, the answer is yes. While some of the tools, props and behaviors may be quite species specific, the same basic concepts and theory of operant conditioning and positive reinforcement can be applied to all species of marine mammals. In addition, the nutritional needs, water quality standards and many other husbandry requirements of marine mammals are very similar for most species. This is one reason that new trainers should take every opportunity to expand their experience and work with any species of marine mammal available to them.

While the basics of training are the same, trainers must also take into account differences in each animal's anatomy, physiology, capabilities and potential when forming individual training plans. To be successful, a trainer should never ask an animal to perform a behavior it is not capable of doing. For example, you would not try to train a dolphin to walk across a stage and sit on a seat, or a sea lion to find an object in the water using only echolocation. Neither species has the physical ability to successfully accomplish the particular task suggested for it. Knowing the abilities and limitations of each animal, then forming a customized training plan, are fundamental steps in the training process, no matter what species is involved.

What is a typical day for a marine mammal trainer?

The specific job requirements of a trainer may vary considerably from one facility to another. However, a typical day for a marine mammal trainer working in zoological park that is open to the public, would be something like this:

Arrive at work in the morning and punch in at the time clock. Check on the health and well-being of the animals in your area. Proceed to the animal food preparation or kitchen facilities. Prepare food for the animals by inspecting, sorting, rinsing and weighing out fish that has been thawing overnight. All food must be fit for human consumption. Store fish in refrigerators. Clean food prep areas and equipment. Feed your animals their first feed of the day with vitamins, as prescribed by the veterinarian. Fill out food and behavior records for each animal. Clean the animals' living areas or habitats. Perform training sessions, shows and demonstrations throughout the day. More records. More cleaning. Spend time interacting with and just getting to know the animals, establishing strong bonds of trust. Help other animal areas as needed. Unload fish delivery trucks as needed. Perform facility repair and maintenance duties within your area as needed. Communicate with your supervisor, director and the veterinarian about your animals and operations. Assist with periodic veterinary examinations as scheduled and as individual animal needs require. Help teach new apprentice trainers how to do their job. Go to meetings to coordinate with other departments in the park. Read and study about new training and husbandry procedures through professional organizations, such as The International Marine Animal Trainers Association (IMATA). Remove frozen fish from freezers and start the thawing process so it will be ready for the next day. Be sure all animals have been fed and cared for completely for the day. Fill out final records. Be sure all areas are secured and safe for the night. Shower and change into clean clothes. Punch out at time clock. Go home and get ready for the next day. Be on call for any unexpected situations or emergencies.

What are typical working conditions?

The working conditions for trainers vary, depending upon the type of facility in which they work. Generally, however, trainers work outdoors in all types of weather. They must be able to lift and carry at least 50 lbs (23 kg). They work around the water, so they need to be strong swimmers, and most facilities require scuba certification. They also need to be able to work and get along well with people, since good training relies heavily on teamwork.

What are typical working hours?

In the United States most trainers (entry through senior level) are employed as hourly staff and work a full-time 40-hour week, with occasional overtime required. Most hourly employees working at US facilities work varying schedules of eight hours per day, five days per week. (Some facilities have adopted work schedules of 10 hours per day, four days per week.) In addition, trainers must be available to respond to unexpected situations as they arise.

Once a trainer advances to supervisor, curator, director or some other managerial position, the required hours may change significantly. Since labor laws within the United States do not generally require supervisory staff to be paid directly for overtime worked, 60 to 80 hour work weeks are not uncommon in the busiest seasons or during births, illnesses, acquisitions, long distance transports, hurricanes and other such situations.

The animals need care and supervision 24 hours per day, seven days per week, 365 days per year. Trainers often work when most other people are off: weekends, holidays, etc.

What are typical pay scales?

The pay rate for trainers is not very high, especially at the entry level. This is primarily true because the high costs associated with properly caring for marine mammals, such as state-of-the-art facilities, life support systems, human quality food and veterinary care, can severely impact company budgets and the ability of many facilities to pay higher salaries. Many zoological facilities are nonprofit institutions and do not generate revenues that allow much opportunity to pay high salaries. In addition, many people are interested in this type of career and want to enter the field. There are usually many more applicants than positions, and a lot of people are willing to volunteer their time and services to gain experience, or just be around these rare animals. Consequently, the law of supply and demand allows for lower wages than in many other, less desirable professions.

Depending upon the location and individual facility, entry level pay for trainers with little or no experience may be between $5.75 (or minimum wage) to $9.00 per hour within the United States. (A few facilities located in areas with the highest cost of living expenses may pay $12.00 per hour or more for entry level positions, but these are rare exceptions.) A senior trainer with eight to 12 years of experience may make $25,000 to $40,000 per year. The pay rate increases with experience, but you will never get rich as a marine mammal trainer. In fact, many trainers work second jobs during the first few years of their careers, just to help pay the bills. As you can see, money is not the primary "reinforcer" for most trainers.

Do employers provide any other benefits?

This is highly dependent upon the individual employer, but many facilities provide health and dental insurance; holiday, vacation and sick pay; as well as 401k and other retirement plans. Some facilities also provide continuing education opportunities, employee parties and other social functions. Zoological parks, aquariums and other institutions that offer guest services, may also offer employee discounts on food and merchandise sold on-site.

What percentage of marine mammal trainers are women?

Twenty years ago, roughly 30% of all marine mammal trainers were women. Since then, far more women than men have shown interest in and are entering this field. Today, female trainers hold approximately 60% of all professional positions worldwide. In the United States, about 70% of all working marine mammal trainers are women. This trend shows no sign of changing in the near future.

What are some of the common advantages and disadvantages of this occupation?

Advantages:

This is highly subjective of course, but for many trainers the best part of this occupation is the ability to work hands-on and develop strong, mutually beneficial relationships with these rare animals. Sharing this experience with other highly motivated people who share a common dedication to the animals, is another valued aspect of this career. In addition, many people derive a great deal of satisfaction from teaching the public about these often misunderstood creatures, and helping to promote awareness, compassion and protection for them and their counterparts (and their critical habitats) in the wild.

Disadvantages:

The fact that there are so few marine mammal facilities in the world, results in some of the most significant disadvantages for people in this profession. These include a lot of competition for the few available jobs and the relatively low pay for highly skilled and educated workers.

Since most communities are lucky to have even one zoological facility with a marine mammal population, changing your place of employment usually requires moving to another town, state or country. In addition, it is a very time consuming job. The animals eat and need care 24/7. Trainers have to be available for any emergency, illness or birth. They usually work when everyone else is off: weekends, holidays, etc. This means that time for their families and themselves often has to come second. This can put a strain on personal relationships.

Occasionally, trainers may have to deal with criticism and accusations from uninformed people who mistakenly believe that these animals are harmed by living in a captive zoological environment. This situation, however, also provides an excellent opportunity to educate the very people who need it the most.

What changes do you foresee in the future for this occupation?

The trend will most likely continue toward increased demand for greater education and advanced degrees. Talented trainers, however, with broad experience, strong husbandry backgrounds, effective communication skills and demonstrated animal sense will always be needed.

Professional organizations, such as the International Marine Animal Trainers Association (IMATA), are strongly promoting the concept of uniform standards and professional accreditation for marine mammal trainers. These would be in addition to the many governmental regulations and professional standards (including staff training and organization) that facilities must already meet.

The demand for entry-level trainers will continue to be low, and is proportionate to the low number of professional positions worldwide. This will most likely continue due to the relatively few zoological institutions in the world that are willing to take on the high costs, political uncertainties and logistical challenges associated with acquiring, properly housing and caring for marine mammals.

Trainers use a variety of tools to achieve success. Here, a trainer uses a target (in this case a foam bead at the end of a bamboo pole) to help guide her sea lion student into a graceful high jump. A second trainee watches the action from his seat on stage.

THE KEYS TO SUCCESS

Now that you have a better idea about what marine mammal trainers do, and the opportunities and challenges of their profession, you should probably be asking yourself a very important question right about now... "Is this the right career choice for me?"

Remember, it can be very difficult to get started as a marine mammal trainer. There are a lot of people who want to do this kind of work and relatively few jobs available. Consequently, there will be a lot of competition and challenges ahead. Obviously, it is not impossible to succeed, but to be one of the fortunate few who actually gets a chance to work professionally with marine mammals, you are going to have to be one of the very best applicants. You are going to have to have and display the qualities and attributes that employers need, seek and desire.

Every institution has its own individual mission, operations and staff requirements. The degree of emphasis on each specific attribute may vary considerably from one facility to another. For example, many facilities provide public shows and educational demonstrations. They may rely heavily on trainers with strong public speaking skills, and teaching and theater arts backgrounds. Some facilities may deal primarily with research and data collection. They may require advanced degrees in biology, animal behavior or other related subjects. Many facilities located near coastlines rescue, rehabilitate and release hundreds of sick, injured and stranded marine mammals back to the wild every year. These institutions may need individuals with strong backgrounds in veterinary care, laboratory analysis and medicine. Many modern marine zoological institutions provide all of these services in one location. They have needs for people with all of these skills and backgrounds. In any case, there are several basic characteristics that seem to be universally desirable. These include education, experience, ability, attitude and commitment.

EDUCATION

This profession is built on a foundation of education. It is one of the fundamental pillars of a strong and meaningful career in marine mammal care and training. To be successful, just getting a diploma, degree or certificate is not enough, however. True understanding and the ability to apply your knowledge must also be acquired.

What kind of education is needed to become a marine mammal trainer?

As stated previously, the operations and needs of each institution may vary greatly from one facility to another. Likewise, the educational requirements set by each facility for its particular training staff may be quite different. Many employers require a minimum of a bachelor's degree in a life science or related field, such as biology, zoology, psychology or animal behavior. Some facilities accept graduates of specialized two-year exotic animal training and management programs, such as the one offered at Moorpark College in Southern California. And, while it is true that some employers only require a high school diploma, a strong understanding of animal biology, behavior, water chemistry, nutrition, veterinary medicine, marine ecology and other related fields is extremely valuable to any person interested in entering and succeeding in this field. It may be vital if they want to progress to a supervisor, curator or director level.

As you develop your own individual educational plan, it is probably wise to begin with the assumption that you are going to need at least a bachelor's degree. You can modify your plan from there as you gather more information and refine your goals. Advanced degrees are becoming increasingly common and are a critical factor at some institutions when considering managerial promotions. Some people are able to continue their formal education and acquire college degrees after they begin working in the field. Keep in mind, this can be a tough road and requires a great deal of discipline and enough financial resources to carry you through to completion.

If you already know of a few marine mammal facilities where you would like to work, you may try contacting them directly and asking what their educational requirements are for their training staff. This information should be available from the companies' Personnel or Human Resources departments and listed on the job descriptions or position announcements for each job title. Job postings and requirements are often listed on company Web sites, which are usually the best places to start your search. Telephone numbers, addresses, Web sites and other contact information for many of the world's marine mammal facilities are presented in the Resource Directory, starting on page 71.

What should I study in high school?

To prepare for the career and college work ahead, high school students should do well in all subjects, but especially math, science and English. Other helpful subjects include public speaking, theater arts, computer science, swimming and creative writing. Where offered, course work and experience in animal husbandry is very helpful.

What colleges and course work are best for this career?

There are many things to consider when choosing the best college or university for you. Each has its own pros and cons depending upon your individual needs, financial resources, location and future goals.

Many trainers have gotten a very good start with a two-year associate's degree or certificate through a specialized curriculum, like Moorpark College's Exotic Animal Training and Management (EATM) Program. On the other hand, if you are interested in going on to perform research or other advanced work, starting out with a master's degree or even a doctorate may be the way to go. For many trainers, a bachelor's degree from their local college or university has served them well throughout their professional careers.

In most cases, a degree specializing in marine mammals is not a prerequisite for a training career. Biology, zoology, psychology, animal behavior and other related subjects are very good choices for this profession and are available at most colleges and universities around the world. On the other hand, those wishing to conduct research or really concentrate their studies, may find a curriculum specializing in marine mammalogy to be quite beneficial.

Facilities that offer public shows, educational programs and training demonstrations often look for applicants with some background and experience in theater arts. In addition, course work and practice in public speaking will be very helpful in most situations.

Contact information for Moorpark College and a few universities that offer specialized courses in marine mammalogy can be found in the Resource Directory, starting on page 127.

EXPERIENCE

No matter what type or level of degree you acquire, education alone will probably not be enough to get you that first full-time trainer job. Along with education, employers put a great deal of value on prior experience when selecting new staff members.

Why do employers put so much emphasis on prior experience?

While a formal education is very important, the only real way to gain the understanding and skills needed to successfully care for and train marine mammals is by working with them under the supervision and tutelage of senior team members. In other words, through practice and hands-on experience. It may take years of on-the-job training before a staff member is able to work independently and train new behaviors on their own.

In addition, many people have unrealistic expectations of what a trainer does. It is a very rewarding career, but it is also a tough job. A trainer's usual daily duties include cleaning, lifting and carrying, preparing fish, cleaning, feeding and training, cleaning, writing records, cleaning, performing in shows or demonstrations, public education and interaction and more cleaning. Employers want to hire people who already have a realistic idea of what the job is like and are ready to take on all of these important responsibilities. No one wants to hire (or work with) someone who is only interested in the fun stuff.

Do internships and volunteer work count?

In most cases interning or volunteering at facilities with marine mammals or other large and/or exotic animals is a great way to demonstrate the type of understanding and commitment needed for this profession. It's also an excellent way to gain real world experience, make contacts and get your foot in the door.

Many trainers acquired their first practical experience by volunteering at local zoos, oceanariums, veterinary hospitals, wildlife rehabilitation centers, animal shelters or horse stables. Often the next step was a paid position as a summer, seasonal or part-time keeper or trainer's assistant.

Many facilities are busiest during the summer or holiday seasons and hire extra entry-level staff at that time. Be sure to apply early, because most facilities like to interview and identify their additional summer staff by early spring.

What is the value of these introductory jobs?

Whether paid or voluntary, these introductory jobs offer several critically important opportunities:

1) to gain practical hands-on experience with large and/or exotic animals
2) to meet and learn from people who are doing the kind of work you desire
3) to experience first hand what it's really like to be an animal professional
4) to see if you truly enjoy this kind of work, or would be happier doing something else
5) to see if you have what it takes to be a success in the animal field, or are better suited to a different career

6) to earn a reputation as a hard working, conscientious and trustworthy member of the team

These jobs also offer the facility's management and training staff an opportunity to evaluate your true qualifications and potential under actual working conditions. Many employers like to hire people they already know and feel comfortable working with. They routinely fill their regular full-time positions with the best candidates from their seasonal and volunteer staff.

ABILITY

Education and experience may get a person hired, but eventually only a demonstrated ability to consistently and effectively do the job will keep that person working and, more important, make them successful in this field. Genuine ability can not be faked. Over time, a person's true nature and aptitude show through. Luck and raw talent may play a role but, most often, success in this field is the result of hard work, careful observation, practice, continued personal study, positive attitude and genuine commitment.

ATTITUDE

A positive and open attitude is an extremely important quality that employers look for when hiring a new marine mammal trainer. Almost everything else can be taught, but attitude must come from within.

The job is often difficult, requiring physical as well as emotional strength. Most job descriptions require a person to work outdoors in all types of weather, to lift and carry heavy objects (usually 50 lbs or more), demonstrate strong swimming skills, be available to work weekends, nights and holidays, be open to flexible work schedules and (very important) to be able to work well with others.

Most jobs require trainers to interact and provide information to the general public. Trainers function as both informal educators and role models. In addition, training and animal care is almost always done as part of a team. A positive, sharing attitude is critical when working in such an environment. A person who loves animals but can't seem to get along with people is not going to do well in this field.

COMMITMENT

People get into this line of work for a variety of reasons, but only those who are truly committed to the animals and the profession stay and advance in it. The marine mammal care and training community is a very small, ethical and proud group of dedicated professionals. Their commitment to the animals runs beyond the physical boundaries of any individual host facility. Trainers communicate frequently with their peers at other institutions, sharing new ideas, information and procedures. If someone is having a health or behavioral problem with one of their animals, they can rely on the knowledge, experience and help of their colleagues around the world.

Professional associations such as the International Marine Animal Trainers Association (IMATA), the Alliance of Marine Mammal Parks and Aquariums (AMMPA) and the American Zoo and Aquarium Association (AZA) help to establish and strengthen these bonds of mutual assistance. Contributing to conference presentations, newsletters, journals and reference books not only helps to advance the community's collective knowledge, it also goes a long way towards enhancing an individual's professional reputation.

In a field dedicated to such high standards and ethics, it should come as no surprise that professional reputations are created and advanced along this well-established network of communication. Commitment to the animals and the profession are the cornerstones of long term success.

A trainer rewards a beluga whale with tactile reinforcement, in this case a gentle rub on the tongue. Positive reinforcement is a fundamental key to successful marine mammal training.

A research volunteer records valuable data during a 24-hour watch, following the birth of a dolphin calf. Many trainers got their start by volunteering at their local zoo, oceanarium, aquarium, re-habilitation center, animal shelter or veterinary clinic.

INSIDE TIPS AND SUGGESTIONS

As a manager of a large marine mammal department, some of my responsibilities included reviewing many applications and resumes, conducting interviews and hiring new staff members. Like most marine mammal supervisors and managers, I had a lot of good applicants vying to fill the few positions that became available every year. Only those candidates who stood out above the others made it to the interview process; even fewer were hired.

This experience has provided me with some valuable insights on what marine mammal facilities and their management teams look for in a successful job candidate. Most of this information is common sense, but you might be surprised at how many, otherwise intelligent and worthy applicants, fail to meet many of these basic criteria.

The following are a few ideas, personal tips and insights that may give you an edge in planning your career, creating a resume, filling out an application and participating in an employment interview.

PLANNING, RESEARCH AND PREPARATION

Gather information

Seek out as much credible information as possible and choose the source carefully. A lot of general information about marine mammals, zoos and oceanariums, and the profession of animal care and training is old and outdated.

Some people who are philosophically opposed to keeping animals in zoological facilities have even produced materials that are exaggerated, false and misleading, in an attempt to discredit them and the animal care profession. The Resource Directory, starting on page 71, is a good place to start your quest for credible data.

Visit marine mammal facilities

Visiting zoological facilities that have marine mammals is an important step in preparing for this career. Most public facilities have trainers or education specialists available to answer your questions after the shows or demonstrations. This kind of interaction can provide a great deal of important information. It can also offer some valuable personal insights into the true nature of the job, from the people who do it every day.

Many of the world's marine mammal facilities are listed in the Resource Directory, beginning on page 71. If there isn't a facility near you, you may want to think about planning a visit to one during your next vacation.

Plan and continue your education

If you are still in high school, stay there and get good grades. While there, plan what you will do next. Talk to guidance counselors and consider the value of a bachelor's degree or higher. In most cases, it is not necessary to major in marine mammalogy or marine biology to become a trainer. As mentioned previously, degrees in broader subjects like biology, zoology, animal behavior and psychology usually meet the requirements of the job description, and offer additional employment options in other fields. Another advantage to this strategy is that most universities and colleges around the world offer these broader courses and degree programs.

For those interested in a more focused curriculum or a marine mammal research career, a few of the colleges and universities in the United States that offer specialized courses in marine mammalogy or exotic animal management are listed in the Resource Directory, starting on page 127.

Stay physically fit

Working with large animals is hard work, and you need to be in good physical shape to do this job. Being able to move quickly, climb ladders, lift and carry heavy objects, swim and scuba dive are just a few of the common job requirements for a marine mammal trainer.

Develop and maintain strong swimming skills

Since marine mammal trainers work in and around water most of the time, it is important to be a strong swimmer. Many facilities conduct swim tests as a condition of employment. The exact requirements vary from facility to facility. If you want to know more about the specific tests performed, you may try contacting the facility directly.

Get Scuba certified

Most marine mammal facilities require their training staff to be scuba certified. Scuba stands for self-contained underwater breathing apparatus. Scuba tanks and equipment allow divers to stay underwater for prolonged periods of time without having to come to the surface to breathe. Scuba divers get the oxygen they need by breathing compressed air from tanks they carry with them, or from long flexible air lines attached to compressors at the surface. In order to use this equipment and perform this activity safely you must take specialized courses and hold a valid certification from an accredited organization such as the Professional Association of

Diving Instructors (PADI) or the National Association of Underwater Instructors (NAUI). Many dive shops, resorts and colleges offer this training and certification. Taking classes in life saving, first-aid and CPR is also recommended.

More information on scuba certification programs is available in the Resource Directory, starting on page 130.

Don't take drugs

In addition to the obvious hazards of endangered health, reduced life span, incarceration and social dysfunction associated with drug use, many employers now require drug testing before they will hire anyone to work with their animals. Many facilities also conduct periodic drug and alcohol checks of their working staff. In order to train and work safely around large animals and water, a person needs to be mentally sharp and alert. Drug and alcohol use is contrary to this goal.

Think hard before you get a tattoo

Most public facilities have dress codes. Policies against employees having visible tattoos is not uncommon. This is especially true of facilities where staff participate in public interactions, educational programs or shows. You may want to reconsider getting that tattoo if it can not be easily covered up by a bathing suit. Getting a tattoo removed can be painful and expensive.

Watch your language

Always be professional when you are interacting with trainers or other animal professionals. Obviously, foul language should be avoided, but there is another seemingly innocent word that many people use incorrectly, and trainers really dislike. That word is "trick." Remember, trainers teach their animals behaviors not tricks. Trainers dislike this word because it falsely implies that the behavior was accomplished through some sort of illusion or deception. Using the word "trick" in this context is not only incorrect, it can be insulting.

Join professional associations

One way to establish professional relationships and gather information and insights into a zoological career is by joining one or more professional associations. These include the International Marine Animal Trainers Association (IMATA), the American Zoo and Aquarium Association (AZA) and the American Association of Zoo Keepers (AAZK). Many of these organizations offer very affordable student memberships.

The Resource Directory has more information about these and other professional zoological associations, starting on page 121.

Get involved in these associations

Once you have joined a professional association and are actively working in the field, you should consider attending one of their conferences. The information and ideas presented in formal papers, posters and workshops are invaluable, and most people find the personal insights and friendships gained through informal interactions just as important and rewarding.

Writing and presenting a paper at a conference is a great way to get involved, but is not something to take lightly. Most people like to gain experience in the process first by helping to coauthor a paper or poster with an experienced veteran.

Once you have this experience, you will have a better idea of the process and what is expected in a formal presentation.

Volunteering to help with a committee is another great way to get started as an active member of an association. Working on a committee will help introduce you to other active members and demonstrate your knowledge, skills and commitment to the community.

Volunteer or intern

Employers like to hire people with prior experience and demonstrated skills. It would be great if you could acquire this type of experience at a facility that has marine mammals, such as an oceanarium, aquarium or rehabilitation center, but any experience with large or exotic animals is highly beneficial. A paid position working for one of these facilities would be great too, but in many cases, the only way to get your initial experience may be to volunteer or intern. Many trainers got their start by becoming a volunteer, intern or docent at their local zoo, veterinary clinic, wildlife rehabilitation center or similar animal operation. Volunteering can be a valuable step along this type of professional career path, and one that can be done while you are still in school, acquiring your formal education.

Apply for seasonal animal positions

For many people, the next logical step in preparing for a career working with marine mammals is to apply for summer or seasonal positions in animal departments at zoos, oceanariums and aquariums. Many of these public facilities hire additional staff within their animal departments to help with the expanded workload associated with increased seasonal attendance. Most of these positions are filled with college students who are studying for a career in this field and are available for work during their summer breaks. Upon graduation, the experience and contacts made during their seasonal employment can really pay off for these individuals. Employers often look to their best seasonal employees first, when searching for someone to fill an open regular full-time entry-level animal position.

Transfer from within

As with most animal-related jobs, the competition for seasonal positions (as described above) is quite strong. Some candidates apply for several years before being selected for one of the few available and coveted positions. In the meantime, another way to get your foot in the door at a zoo, marine park or aquarium, may be to also apply for work in one of the facility's nonanimal-related departments. Quite a few zoological professionals began their careers as seasonal or part-time employees in food service, merchandise, guest relations or similar departments before successfully transferring into an animal-related position. While this strategy will not substitute for hands-on animal experience, it will allow you to establish yourself as a dedicated employee and learn firsthand about the hiring practices and job requirements within the company. This tactic will also allow you to make a little money while still in school or college, acquiring your formal education. Even though this type of work may not be your first choice of employment, it's important to stay focused on the work at hand, and use this opportunity to do a good job for the people who initially hire you. You'll need a positive recommendation from your supervisor when you are ready to apply for that open position in an animal department.

THE RESUME AND APPLICATION

Your resume and application offer you your first (and sometimes only) opportunity to demonstrate your value to a potential employer. You might have an outstanding formal education and work history, but unless you can accurately and concisely represent it on paper, you may never get another chance to show them what a great employee you can be.

Over the years I have reviewed quite a large number of resumes and applications and have participated in many hiring interviews. Successful applicants always stood out (in a positive way) from the rest of the crowd. Something about the way they presented themselves made us want to give them a chance, and let them show us what they could do for our team. This is what you are trying to achieve in your resume and interview.

Use the proper format

Resumes come in many styles. Be sure yours is well-organized, clean, clear, concise and professional. If you produce your own resume, you might want to get help from a book or computer program written for this purpose, to help you maintain professional formatting, style and appearance. Be sure to have someone who writes well review your resume before you make your final copies.

Spelling counts

Check and double-check your spelling, punctuation, grammar and sentence structure. With a large stack of resumes to review, the ones that stand out by missing this basic concept are often the first to hit the reject file. It is reasonable to assume that if someone is sloppy on their application and resume, they are probably sloppy in their other work habits as well. After you are sure it is perfect, have someone else review it again. It's easy to miss an incomplete sentence or a misspelled word.

Be professional

Don't get too cute with your resume. While you want it to stand out, you do not want it to jump up and down and scream. Avoid obvious and childish attention grabbers like overly boastful statements, hard to read fonts, strange graphics or outlandish paper choices. Remember, training is a profession. Be professional.

Be honest

People naturally want to fill their resumes with as much great stuff as possible, but be careful. Don't exaggerate or embellish your skills, experience or accomplishments too much.

Some people may not be proud of certain things in their past. If an application asks for information that you would rather avoid, be cautious and don't lie. Most employers are very careful to only ask for information they have a legal right to know. Being caught in a lie is a sure way to get disqualified or fired later.

Follow directions

Read the application and all instructions carefully and completely *before* filling it out. This will help prevent mistakes and placement errors. When you are ready and have all your thoughts and responses organized, follow all directions, and fill out the form completely.

Try to get more than one copy of an application form. It's not a good idea to submit applications where obvious mistakes have been crossed out or touched up with correction fluid. Having a second clean application form on hand will help prevent having to submit a messy application.

Prepare your references

Have a list of personal and professional references prepared and ready to present if requested. Normally, a list of references is not automatically submitted with an application. It is usually a good idea, however, to write at the end of your resume, "References available upon request." Be sure to contact the people you want to include on the list before finalizing it. Let them know that you would like to list them as references, and get their permission before giving their names and contact information to anyone.

Sometimes a picture really is worth a thousand words

Some aspects of this job are like theater. Facilities that offer public shows, demonstrations or tours may be interested in maintaining a certain look for their performers. Some companies actually refer to their employees as "cast members."

Most employers do not ask for photos, but many would love to have one. If you don't have a problem with it, go ahead and send along a photo (or video) of you training your favorite animal or working with some school kids. It just may be the thing that sets your application apart from all the rest.

Note: Some laws and company policies do not allow this. Be sure to ask the company's Personnel or Human Resources department if you can include a photo or video with your resume before you send it.

Be sure you are qualified

Before submitting an application or resume for a specific job, be sure you meet the minimum qualifications for that position. You should be able to get this information from the facility's Personnel or Human Resources department. These requirements may also be listed on job announcements posted on company bulletin boards and Web sites or published in newspapers and professional newsletters. In most cases, it's not a good idea to waste an employer's time by submitting an application when you do not possess the basic qualifications for the position. In some cases, it may even hurt your chances for future openings.

Don't badger

Once you submit your application or resume, don't badger or harass the employer with too many questions about the status of your paperwork. If you mail in your materials, it may be a good idea to call and verify that they have arrived. You can also ask if it is appropriate for you to call back to track the status of the application and, if so, how often. Making too many calls or e-mail inquiries will probably not help your chances. Remember, people who work around animals need to have patience. It's a good idea to demonstrate that you are a patient and considerate person right from the beginning.

THE INTERVIEW

With hard work, preparation and a little luck, your application and resume will earn you the opportunity to really show an employer what a great addition to their team you can be. In most cases, this means an appointment for an interview. Most interviews are conducted in person, at the place of business. In some cases, such as where long distances are a factor, initial interviews may be conducted over the telephone.

Do some detective work

Be well-prepared before your interview appointment. Learn as much as possible about the prospective facility's mission, operations, staff, shows, animal species, pay scale, etc., before applying, and especially before starting an interview. The company's own Web site may be the best place to begin this information search. If you've never been to the facility before, try to make a personal visit a few days before your interview to gather more information and get a feel for the place. If the job will require relocating to a new area, it's a good idea to do some research on local housing and living costs. These expenses may vary considerably from one region or community to another.

Come prepared

Have everything you need with you for the interview. A portfolio, brief case or small book bag may be beneficial. You should take your completed application form, several copies of your resume, your list of references, original social security card, and proof of identification and citizenship with you. In some cases, you may need copies of your high school and college transcripts, work history and other support documents.

It's a good idea to write down any questions you might have about the job or facility so you can quickly refer to them if the opportunity arises. Most employment interviews end by asking the candidate if they have any questions. If you have questions, this is the best time to bring them up. In addition, being ready with a few well-thought-out inquiries shows your level of preparation and commitment to the position.

Get some rest

Get a good night's sleep before your appointment. You want to be well-rested, sharp and alert for your interview.

Appearance counts

Remember, this is a business appointment. Come clean, well-groomed and dressed in proper business attire.

Be on time

Get to your appointment a little early, but don't expect the interviewer to drop what they are doing and start your interview 20 minutes ahead of schedule. Use this time to get comfortable and relax. If the interview is by telephone, be sure to be by the phone with all your notes and paperwork well before the appointed time.

Listen carefully and follow all instructions

You may be given more paperwork to fill out or asked to go to some other location. Pay attention to all instructions and directions.

Be courteous to everyone

You never know to whom you are talking. The person meeting you at the gate may be a trainer, a security guard, the personnel director, your future boss or the chief executive officer. No matter who it is, everyone deserves respect, and word travels fast when someone is rude or impolite. Be honest, polite and confident, but not aggressive. During the interview, feel free to ask a few questions, at the appropriate times, but don't come off like a lawyer cross-examining a witness.

Be open to new ideas and methods

If you have actual animal work experience, don't keep saying, "At my old facility we did it this way." Remember, there is more than one right way to do just about everything. If you get hired, they'll expect you to learn and do things their way first. Who knows, maybe the way your old employer did some things really was better. You'll get your chance to demonstrate that, once you've proven yourself.

Be businesslike

Remember, it is very expensive to take care of marine mammals properly. State-of-the-art facilities, life support systems, human quality food and 24-hour care are just some of the high cost factors involved. In order to pay for these necessary expenses, most employers rely on revenue generated by the visiting public through tickets sales, food and merchandise receipts or direct donations. Demonstrating that you understand the value of proper guest service, budget control and protecting company assets shows a high degree of professionalism and may really set you apart from the crowd.

End on a positive note

Most trainers believe you should always end a training session on a positive note. The same can be said of an employment interview. No matter how you feel the interview went, stay positive. Always thank the interviewer for their time and consideration.

Be patient

Again, remember, patience is an important quality of any trainer or animal care professional. Before you leave the interview, you should ask about the next step in the hiring process. Find out if you are to call back at some point for their decision, or just wait for their call. Follow any instructions regarding the notification process. In some cases it may be okay to call for occasional updates about the status of the position. Most employers, however, don't appreciate a lot of unnecessary calls or e-mails. Most will call and notify everyone who was interviewed, once they have made their decision.

Within a day or two of the interview, be sure to write a short note to thank the interviewer(s) and anyone who may have gone out of their way to help you.

SAMPLE INTERVIEW QUESTIONS

There is no standard set of interview questions used by all marine mammal facilities or management teams. The questions presented below, however, are probably pretty typical. Take some time and try answering these for yourself. There aren't any right or wrong answers. The questions are designed to assess a candidate's experience, skill and qualifications.

Even if these particular questions are not asked in your interview, reviewing this list will help you better understand the requirements of an entry-level marine mammal trainer position. This exercise will also help you prepare for the interview process and assess your qualifications. It's much better to identify any potential weaknesses now, and work towards correcting them, than to discover your areas of concern during an actual interview.

Sample interview questions for an entry-level marine mammal trainer position:

1. Have you read and understand the posted job description?
2. Do you have any questions regarding the salary and compensation?
3. Are you able to perform the job as described?
4. Do you have any limitations that would prevent you from meeting all of the job requirements?
5. What kind of animal care or training experience do you have? (With what kinds of animals?)
6. Do you understand the basic concepts of operant conditioning?
7. Why do you think you would work well with our animals?
8. What behaviors (if any) have you trained and are most proud of?
9. What do you think is the biggest lesson you've learned so far working with animals?
10. How would you handle a situation with an aggressive animal?
11. Do you have any experience in public speaking or performing?
12. Are you comfortable speaking and performing in front of large groups?
13. Do you have any problem working weekends, holidays, nights or overtime?
14. How would you handle a problem with a fellow employee?
15. What do you see yourself doing in two years? five years? 10 years?
16. What do you feel is the most important function of a zoo or oceanarium?
17. How do you feel about animals collected from the wild and maintained in zoos and oceanariums?
18. Are you a strong swimmer?

19. Are you Scuba certified?
20. How often do you Scuba dive?
21. Can you lift and carry 50 lbs (23 kg)?
22. Can you safely work and get around in our animal areas?

Another common question that many interviewers ask is, "What is your favorite animal?"

Sounds like an easy one, doesn't it? Before you answer, think about this. It's fine to prefer one or two particular animal species. Most people have preferences. But, unless you just don't want to work with any animals other than dolphins or killer whales, be sure to let the employer know that you would be happy and excited to work with any of their marine mammals.

Everyone loves dolphins. They are great animals and have received a lot of press. It takes someone who has done their homework to realize that sea lions, harbor seals, walruses and other, less high profile, species are just as rewarding and fun to work with. In addition, the basic knowledge and skills needed to care for and train cetaceans are very similar to those required for other marine mammals. Therefore, working with any type of marine mammal offers invaluable experience.

It's also important to understand that there are relatively few cetaceans housed in zoological facilities around the world, compared to the much larger number of pinnipeds and other marine mammal species. Consequently, there are far fewer jobs working with cetaceans than with other marine mammals. Many zoos have sea lions and harbor seals in their collections, for example, but only a relative few have dolphins.

Most dolphin and killer whale trainers, I know, started out working with seals, sea lions, other marine mammals or terrestrial animals. If they had decided during their first interview that they were only interested in working with dolphins or whales, they would probably never have gotten that first critical job. Besides, once many of these trainers began working with pinnipeds, otters, polar bears and other animals, they discovered that they liked them so much, that these species actually became their new favorite animals.

These four young walrus calves will have to wait about another year before their characteristic tusks begin to show. Even at this early age animals can benefit from modern methods of training and behavioral enrichment.

AFTERWORD

The ideas and suggestions presented in this book are primarily intended for people just starting out upon their own career path, that is for those individuals trying to fulfill their personal dream of becoming a marine mammal trainer or care specialist. One of the primary goals of this guide is to present a realistic picture, including the pros and cons, of this unique profession. Given that information, different readers will make different decisions.

Some people may come to the conclusion that the career and lifestyle of a marine mammal trainer is not what they thought it was after all. They may decide to continue searching for other careers more suited to their own particular interests, goals and desires. Others may want to continue pursuing a career within the zoological community, but perhaps one more acutely focused on education, conservation, research or veterinary medicine. For many folks, just volunteering a few days a month at a local zoo, aquarium or wildlife rescue facility satisfies their desire to work around wild or exotic animals, while still allowing them the opportunity to pursue other, more conventional nonanimal-related careers. For these individuals, becoming a volunteer or docent offers them the chance to experience the best of both worlds.

If, after all this, you are one of the readers who still wants to pursue your dream of becoming a full-time professional marine mammal trainer, then congratulations and welcome. Yes, competition is tough and getting that first job will be a challenge, but don't get discouraged. If you aren't selected for one of those first few jobs, keep trying. Learn and grow from each experience. Often, the difference between success and failure is having the courage, determination, patience and foresight to look at each small set back as an opportunity. Every time you fill out an application or participate in an employment interview you can learn something new about yourself. You can use these insights to recognize areas where you can grow and work to improve them and apply each lesson to the next challenge.

Remember, every successful marine mammal professional was, at some point in their career, right where you are right now…working hard to turn their own personal dream into a reality.

Good luck and enjoy the adventure!

RESOURCE DIRECTORY

It is often said that information is power. Knowing where to find accurate and relevant information is vital to every successful career. There is a vast amount of data, insight and opinion about marine mammals and the community that cares for and trains them. Not all of it is accurate or useful. Sorting through this mountain of information can be a daunting task. The remainder of this book is dedicated to that challenge.

The resource material and contact information compiled on the following pages should prove helpful to anyone involved in marine mammal care and training, from novices to veterans.

ZOOLOGICAL FACILITIES WITH MARINE MAMMALS

The following is a list of zoological facilities around the world that house and care for marine mammals. Information about each facility includes its name, address and, where available, its telephone number, fax number, e-mail address and Web site. The common names of marine mammal species regularly housed at each facility are also included.

Facilities within the United States of America are listed in alphabetical order by state, starting on the next page. Listings for facilities outside the US begin on page 95. International listings are arranged in alphabetical order by country.

United States of America – by State

ALASKA -

Alaska Sealife Center
PO Box 1329
Seward, AK 99664
USA
Phone: +907-224-6300
Fax: +907-224-6320
Web site: http://www.alaskasealife.org
Stellar Sea Lions, Harbor Seals

CALIFORNIA -

Aquarium of the Pacific
100 Aquarium Way
Long Beach, CA 90802
USA
Phone: +562-951-3100
Fax: +562-951-1629
Web site: http://www.aquariumofpacific.org
California Sea Lions, Harbor Seals, Sea Otters

Friends of the Sea Lion Marine Mammal Center
20612 Laguna Canyon Road
Laguna Beach, CA 92651
USA
California Sea Lions, Harbor Seals

Long Marine Laboratory / UCSC
100 Shaffer Road
Santa Cruz, CA 95060
USA
Web site: http://ims.ucsc.edu
Bottlenose Dolphins, California Sea Lions, Northern Elephant
Seals, Harbor Seals, Sea Otters

Los Angeles Zoo
5333 Zoo Drive
Los Angeles, CA 90027
USA
Phone: +323-644-4200
Fax: +323-662-9786
Web site: http://www.lazoo.org
California Sea Lions, Grey Seals, Polar Bears

Marine Mammal Care Center at Fort MacArthur
3601 South Gaffey Street
San Pedro, CA 90731
USA
Phone: +310-548-5677
Fax: +310-548-6394
Web site: http://www.mar3ine.org
California Sea Lions, Harbor Seals, Northern Elephant Seals,
Northern Fur Seals

The Marine Mammal Center
Marin Headlands
1065 Fort Cronkhite
Sausalito, CA 94965
USA
Phone: +415-289-7325
Fax: +415-289-7333
Web site: http://www.marinemammalcenter.org
California Sea Lions, Harbor Seals, Northern Elephant Seals,
Northern Fur Seals, Sea Otters

Monterey Bay Aquarium
886 Cannery Row
Monterey, CA 93940
USA
Phone: +831-648-4800
Web site: http://www.mbayaq.org
Sea Otters

Morro Bay Aquarium
595 Embarcadero
Morro Bay, CA 93442-2217
USA
Phone: +805-772-7647
Fax: +805-772-7683
E-mail: mbaquarium@thegrid.net
California Sea Lions, Harbor Seals

Moss Landing Marine Lab
8272 Moss Landing Road
Moss Landing, CA 95039
USA
Phone: +831-633-5642
Fax: +831-663-0805
California Sea Lions

Ocean World
304 Highway 101, S.
Crescent City, CA 95531
USA
Phone: +707-464-4900
Fax: +707-464-8318
California Sea Lions, Harbor Seals

Santa Barbara Zoo
500 Ninos Drive
Santa Barbara, CA 93103
USA
Phone: +805-962-5339
California Sea Lions

Science Applications International Corp. (SAIC)
3990 Old Town Ave. Suite 105A
San Diego, CA 92106
USA
Phone: +619-686-5700
Fax: +619-294-8795
Bottlenose Dolphins, Beluga Whales, California Sea Lions

Sea World San Diego
500 Sea World Drive
San Diego, CA 92109
USA
Phone: +619-225-3217
Fax: +619-226-3964
Web site: http://www.seaworld.com
Killer Whales, Bottlenose Dolphins, Pilot Whales, California Sea
Lions, Walruses, Harbor Seals, West Indian Manatees, Sea Otters,
Polar Bears

Six Flags Marine World
2001 Marine World Parkway
Vallejo, CA 94589
USA
Phone: +707-644-4000
Fax: +707-644-0241
Web site: http://www.sixflags.com/marineworld
Bottlenose Dolphins, California Sea Lions, Walruses, Harbor Seals

US Navy Marine Mammal Program
Space and Naval Warfare Systems Center, San Diego
Biosciences Division (Code D35)
53560 Hull Street
San Diego, CA 92152
USA
Phone: +619-553-5252
Fax: +619-553-2678
Web site: http://agena.spawar.navy.mil
Bottlenose Dolphins, Beluga Whales, California Sea Lions

Zoological Society of San Diego
PO Box 551
San Diego, CA 92112-0551
USA
Phone: +619-231-1515
Fax: +619-231-0249
Web site: http://www.sandiegozoo.org
California Sea Lions, Polar Bears

COLORADO -

Denver Zoological Gardens
2300 Steele Street
Denver, CO 80205-4899
USA
Phone: +303-376-4900
Fax: +303-376-4901
California Sea Lions, Harbor Seals, Polar Bears

Ocean Journey
700 Water Street
Denver, CO 80211
USA
Phone: +303-561-4450
Fax: +303-561-4597
Web site: http://www.oceanjourney.org
Sea Otters

CONNECTICUT -

Maritime Aquarium at Norwalk
10 North Water Street
Norwalk, CT 06379
USA
Phone: +203-852-0700
Harbor Seals

Mystic Marinelife Aquarium
55 Coogan Blvd.
Mystic, CT 06379
USA
Phone: +860-572-5955
Fax: +860-572-5969
Web site: http://www.mysticaquarium.org
Beluga Whales, Stellar Sea Lions, California Sea Lions, Northern
Fur Seals, Harbor Seals

FLORIDA -

Clearwater Marine Aquarium
249 Windward Passage
Clearwater, FL 33767
USA
Phone: +727-441-1790
Fax: +727-442-9466
Web site: http://www.cmaquarium.org
Bottlenose Dolphins

Discovery Cove
6000 Discovery Cove Way
Orlando, FL 32821
USA
Phone: +407-370-1428
Web site: http://www.discoverycove.com
Bottlenose Dolphins

The Dolphin Connection
Hawk's Cay Resort
61 Hawk's Cay Blvd.
Duck Key, FL 33050
USA
Phone: +305-743-7000 ext.1220
Web site: http://www.dolphinconnection.com
Bottlenose Dolphins

Dolphin Cove
PO Box 870
Key Largo, FL 33037
USA
Phone: +305-451-4060
Fax: +305-451-4021
Web site: http://www.dolphinscove.com
                http://www.dolphinsplus.com
Bottlenose Dolphins

Dolphin Research Center
58901 Overseas Highway
Grassy Key, FL 33050-6019
USA
Phone: +305-289-1121
Fax: +305-743-7627
Web site: http://www.dolphins.org
Bottlenose Dolphins, California Sea Lions

Epcot – The Living Seas
2020 N. Avenue of the Stars
Lake Buena Vista, FL 32830-1000
USA
Web site: http://www.disney.com
Bottlenose Dolphins, West Indian Manatees

Gulf World Marine Park
15412 Front Beach Road
Panama City Beach, FL 32413
USA
Phone: +850-234-5271
Fax: +850-235-8957
Web site: http://www.gulfworldmarinepark.com
Bottlenose Dolphins, California Sea Lions, Harbor Seals

Lowry Park Zoo
1101 West Sligh Avenue
Tampa, FL 33604
USA
Phone: +813-935-8552
Fax: +813-935-9486
Web site: http://www.lowryparkzoo.com
West Indian Manatees

Marineland of Florida
9600 Ocean Shore Blvd.
St. Augustine, FL 32080
USA
Phone: +904-460-1275
Website: http://www.marineland.net
Bottlenose Dolphins

Miami Seaquarium
4400 Rickenbacker Causeway
Miami, FL 33149
USA
Phone: +305-361-5705
Web site: http://www.miamiseaquarium.com
Killer Whale, Bottlenose Dolphins, Pacific White-sided Dolphins

Mote Marine Laboratory and Aquarium
1600 Ken Thompson Parkway
Sarasota, FL 34236
USA
Phone: +941-388-4441
Web site: http://www.mote.org
West Indian Manatees

Sea World Orlando
7007 Sea World Drive
Orlando, FL 32821
USA
Phone: +407-351-3600
Web site: http://www.seaworld.com
Killer Whales, Bottlenose Dolphins, False Killer Whales,
California Sea Lions, Walruses, Harbor Seals, West Indian
Manatees, Polar Bears

Theater Of The Sea
84721 Overseas Highway
Islamorada, FL 33036
USA
Phone: +305-664-2431
Fax: +305-664-8162
Web site: http://www.theaterofthesea.com
Bottlenose Dolphins, California Sea Lions

HAWAII -

The Dolphin Institute / Kewalo Basin Marine Mammal Lab
420 Ward Ave., Suite 212
Honolulu, HI 96814
USA
Phone: + 808-593-2211
Web site: http://www.dolphin-institute.org
Bottlenose Dolphins

Dolphin Quest - Hawaii
c/o Hilton Waikoloa Village
69-425 Waikoloa Beach Drive
Waikoloa, HI 96738
USA
Phone: +808-886-1234
Fax: +808-886-7030
E-mail: dqhi@dolphinquest.org
Web site: http://www.dolphinquest.org
Bottlenose Dolphins

Dolphin Quest - Oahu
5000 Kahala Avenue
Honolulu, HI 96816
USA
Phone: +808-737-2292
Fax: +808-737-8311
E-mail: dqoahu@dolphinquest.org
Web site: http://www.dolphinquest.org
Bottlenose Dolphins

Sea Life Park Hawaii
41-202 Kalanianaole Highway
Waimanalo, HI 96795
USA
Phone: +808-259-7933
Bottlenose Dolphins, California Sea Lions, Harbor Seals,
Hawaiian Monk Seals

ILLINOIS -

Chicago Zoological Society
Brookfield Zoo
3300 S. Golf Road
Brookfield, IL 60513-1099
USA
Phone: +708-485-2200
Fax: +708-485-3532
Web site: http://www.brookfieldzoo.org
Bottlenose Dolphins, California Sea Lions, Walruses, Harbor Seals

Lincoln Park Zoo
2200 Cannon Drive
Chicago, IL 60614
USA
Phone: +312-742-2000
Fax: +312-742-2137
Harbor Seals, Grey Seals, Polar Bears

Miller Park Zoo
1020 South Morris Avenue
Bloomington, IL 61701-6351
USA
Phone: +309-434-2250
Fax: +309-434-2823
California Sea Lions, Harbor Seals

Shedd Aquarium
1200 South Lake Shore Drive
Chicago, IL 60605
USA
Phone: +312-939-2426
Fax: +312-939-2216
Web site: http://www.sheddaquarium.org
Beluga Whales, Pacific White-sided Dolphins, Harbor Seals, Sea Otters

INDIANA -

Fort Wayne Children's Zoo
3411 Sherman Blvd.
Fort Wayne, IN 46808
USA
Phone: +219-482-4610
Fax: +219-483-6565
California Sea Lions

Indianapolis Zoo
1200 W. Washington St.
Indianapolis, IN 46222-4500
USA
Phone: +317-630-2001
Fax: +317-630-5153
Web site: http://www.indyzoo.com
Bottlenose Dolphins, California Sea Lions, Walruses, Harbor
Seals, Polar Bears

IOWA -

Blank Park Zoo
7401 S.W. Ninth Street
Des Moines, IA 50315
USA
Phone: +515-285-2676
California Sea Lions, Harbor Seals

LOUISIANA -

Aquarium of the Americas
1 Canal Street
New Orleans, LA 70130
USA
Phone: +504-565-3033
Fax: +504-565-3034
Web site: http://www.auduboninstitute.org
Sea Otters

Audubon Zoological Gardens
PO Box 4327
New Orleans, LA 70178-4327
USA
Phone: +504-861-2537
Fax: +504-866-0819
Web site: http://www.auduboninstitute.org
California Sea Lions

MARYLAND -

National Aquarium in Baltimore
501 E. Pratt Street, Pier 3
Baltimore, MD 21202
Phone: +410-576-3800
Fax: +410-576-1080
Web site: http://www.aqua.org
Bottlenose Dolphins, Harbor Seals, Grey Seals

MASSACHUSETTS -

New England Aquarium
Central Wharf
Boston, MA 02110
Phone: +617-973-5200
Fax: +617-723-6207
Web site: http://www.neaq.org
California Sea Lions, Harbor Seals, Sea Otters

MINNESOTA -

Minnesota Zoological Gardens
13000 Zoo Blvd.
Apple Valley, MN 55124
USA
Phone: +612-431-9200
Fax: +612-431-9300
Web site: http:// www.mnzoo.org
Bottlenose Dolphins

MISSOURI -

Saint Louis Zoo
Forest Park
St. Louis, MO 63110
USA
Phone: +314-781-0900
Fax: +314-647-7969
California Sea Lions

MISSISSIPPI -

Marine Animal Productions
PO Box 4078
Gulfport, MS 39502-4078
USA
Phone: +228-864-2511
Fax: +228-863-3673
Web site: http://www.dolphinsrus.com
Bottlenose Dolphins, California Sea Lions

NEBRASKA -

Folsom Children's Zoo
1222 SO 27th
Lincoln, NE 68502
USA
Phone: +402-475-6741
Fax: +402-475-6742
Harbor Seals

NEVADA -

Mirage Dolphin Environment
3400 Las Vegas Blvd.
Las Vegas, NV 89109
USA
Phone: +702-791-7588
Fax: +702-792-7684
Bottlenose Dolphins

NEW JERSEY -

Jenkinson's Aquarium
300 Ocean Avenue
Point Pleasant Beach, NJ 08742
USA
Phone: +732-899-1212
Web site: http://www.jenkinsons.com/aquarium
Harbor Seals

New Jersey State Aquarium
1 Riverside Drive
Camden, NJ 08103
USA
Phone: +856-365-0352
Web site: http://www.njaquarium.org
Harbor Seals, Grey Seals

NEW MEXICO -

Albuquerque Biological Park
903 Tenth Street SW
Albuquerque, NM 87102
USA
Phone: +505-764-6200
Fax: +505-848-7192
Web site: http://www.cabq.gov/biopark
California Sea Lions, Harbor Seals, Polar Bears

NEW YORK -

Aquarium of Niagara
701 Whirlpool Street
Niagara Falls, NY 14301
USA
Phone: +716-285-3575
Fax: +716-285-8513
Web site: http://www.aquariumofniagara.org
California Sea Lions, Harbor Seals

New York Aquarium
Boardwalk and West 8th Street
Brooklyn, NY 11224
USA
Phone: +718-265-3474
Web site: http://www.nyaquarium.com
Bottlenose Dolphins, Beluga Whales, California Sea Lions,
Walruses, Northern Fur Seals, Harbor Seals, Grey Seals, Sea
Otters

The Utica Zoo
99 Steele Hill Road
Utica, NY 13501
USA
Phone: +315-738-0472
Fax: +315-738-0475
Web site: http://www.uticazoo.org
California Sea Lions

NORTH CAROLINA -

North Carolina Zoo
4401 Zoo Parkway
Asheboro, NC 27205
USA
Phone: +800-488-0444
Web site: http://www.nczoo.org
California Sea Lions, Harbor Seals, Polar Bears

OHIO -

Cleveland Metroparks Zoo
3900 Wildlife Way
Cleveland, OH 44109
USA
Phone: +216-661-6500
Web site: http://www.clemetzoo.com
California Sea Lions, Harbor Seals, Polar Bears

Columbus Zoo and Aquarium
9990 Riverside Drive Box 400
Powell, OH 43065
USA
Phone: +614-645-3550
Web site: http://www.colszoo.org
West Indian Manatee

The Toledo Zoo
PO Box 140130
Toledo, OH 43614
USA
Phone: +419-385-5721
Web site: http://www.toledozoo.org
Harbor Seals, Grey Seals, Polar Bears

OKLAHOMA -

The Oklahoma City Zoo
2101 NE 50th Street
Oklahoma City, OK 73111
USA
Phone: +405-424-3344
Web site: http://www.okczoo.com
California Sea Lions

OREGON -

Oregon Coast Aquarium
2820 S.E. Ferry Slip Road
Newport, OR 97365
USA
Phone: +541-867-3474
Web site: http://www.aquarium.org
Sea Otters, California Sea Lions

Oregon Zoo
4001 SW Canyon Road
Portland, OR 97221
USA
Phone: +503-226-1561
Web site: http://www.oregonzoo.org
Stellar Sea Lions, Sea Otters, Polar Bears

PENNSYLVANIA -

The Pittsburgh Zoo & PPG Aquarium
One Wild Place
Pittsburgh, PA 15206
USA
Phone: +412-665-3640
                +800-474-4966
Web site: http://www.pittsburghzoo.com
Amazon River Dolphins, California Sea Lions

SOUTH CAROLINA -

Riverbanks Zoo and Garden
500 Wildlife Pkwy
Columbia, SC 29202
USA
Phone: +803-779-8717
Fax: +803-253-6381
Web site: http://www.riverbanks.org
California Sea Lions, Harbor Seals, Polar Bears

TENNESSEE -

Memphis Zoo and Aquarium
2000 Prentiss Place
Memphis, TN 38112
USA
Phone: +901-333-6500
Fax: +901-333-6501
Web site: http://www.memphiszoo.org
California Sea Lions

TEXAS -

El Paso Zoo
4001 E. Paisano
El Paso, TX 79905-4223
USA
Phone: +915-521-1850
Fax: +915-521-1857
California Sea Lions

Moody Gardens
One Hope Blvd.
Galveston, TX 77554
USA
Phone: +800-582-4673
California Sea Lions

Sea World San Antonio
10500 Sea World Drive
San Antonio, TX 78251
USA
Phone: +973-523-3600
Fax: +973-523-3299
Web site: http://www.seaworld.com
Killer Whales, Bottlenose Dolphins, Beluga Whales, Pacific
White-sided Dolphins, California Sea Lions, Walruses, Harbor
Seals, Stellar Sea Lions

VIRGINIA -

Virginia Marine Science Museum
717 General Booth Blvd.
Virginia Beach, VA 23451
USA
Phone: +757-425-3474
Fax: +757-437-6338
Web site: http://www.vmsm.com
Harbor Seals

WASHINGTON -

Point Defiance Zoo & Aquarium
5400 N. Pearl Street
Tacoma, WA 98407
USA
Phone: +253-404-3671
Fax: +253-591-5448
Beluga Whales, California Sea Lions, Walruses, Harbor Seals, Sea Otters, Polar Bears

Seattle Aquarium
1483 Alaskan Way, Pier 59
Seattle, WA 98101-2059
USA
Phone: +206-386-4348
Fax: +206-386-4328
Northern Fur Seals, Harbor Seals, Sea Otters

WASHINGTON DC -

Smithsonian National Zoological Park
3001 Connecticut Avenue NW
Washington, DC 20008
USA
Phone: +202-673-4809
Fax: +202-673-4766
California Sea Lions, Grey Seals

WISCONSIN -

Oceans of Fun
10001 W. Bluemound Road
Milwaukee, WI 53226
USA
Phone: +414-256-2503
Fax: +414-256-5410
Web site: http://www.oceansoffun.org
California Sea Lions, Harbor Seals

International – by Country

ANGUILLA -

Dolphin Fantaseas - Anguilla
PO Box 1472
The Valley
Anguilla, BWI
Phone: + 264-497-7946
Fax: + 264-497-0650
E-mail: Anguilla@dolphinfantaseas.com
Web site: http://www.dolphinfantaseas.com
Bottlenose Dolphins

ANTIGUA -

Dolphin Fantaseas - Antigua
PO Box 306
St Johns
Antigua, WI
Phone: + 268-562-7946
Fax: + 268-562-3646
E-mail: Antigua@dolphinfantaseas.com
Web site: http://www.dolphinfantaseas.com
Bottlenose Dolphins

ARGENTINA -

Mundo Marino S.A.
Avenida Decima No. 157
7105 San Clemente del Tuyu
Provincia de Buenos Aires
Argentina
Phone: + 2252-430-300
Fax: + 2252-421-501
E-mail: mundomar@satlink.com.ar
Web site: http://www.mundomarino.com.ar/
Killer Whales, Bottlenose Dolphins, Southern Sea lions, Southern
Elephant Seals, South American Fur Seals

AUSTRALIA -

Melbourne Zoological Gardens
PO Box 74
Parkville, Victoria 3052
Australia
Phone: + 3-03-9285-9300
Fax: + 3-03-9285-9300
Web site: http://www.zoo.org.au
Sub-Antarctic Fur Seals, South African Fur Seals

Pet Porpoise Pool Pty Ltd.
PO Box 532
Coffs Harbor 2450
N.S.W.
Australia
Phone: + 652-2164
Fax: + 650-0264
Bottlenose Dolphins, California Sea Lions, Australian Sea Lions,
New Zealand Fur Seals, Leopard Seals

Sea World Australia
PO Box 190 Surfers Paradise
Gold Coast Queensland 4217
Australia
Phone: + 07-5588-2222
Fax: + 07-5591-1056
Web site: http://www.seaworld.com.au
Bottlenose Dolphins, Indo-Pacific Humpback Dolphins, California
Sea Lions, Harbor Seals, South African Fur Seals, Sub-Antarctic
Furs Seals, Australian Sea Lions, New Zealand Fur Seals

Sydney Aquarium
Aquarium Pier
Darling Harbour
N.S.W. 2000
Australia
Phone: + 02-9262-2300
Fax: + 02-9262-2385
Harbor Seals, South African Fur Seals, New Zealand Fur Seals,
Sub-Antarctic Furs Seals

Taronga Zoo
PO Box 20
Mosman
N.S.W. 2088
Australia
Phone: + 02-9978-4764
Fax: + 02-9978-4613
Web site: http://www.zoo.nsw.gov.au
Harbor Seals, New Zealand Fur Seals, South African Fur Seals,
Australian Sea Lions, Leopard Seals

Underwater World, Mooloolaba
PO Box 511
Mooloolaba, Queensland 4557
Australia
Phone: + 07-5444-8488
Fax: + 07-5444-8515
Web site: http://www.underwaterworld.com.au
New Zealand Fur Seals, South African Fur Seals, Australian Sea
Lions

BAHAMAS -

Dolphin Encounters
PO Box N-7448
Nassau
Bahamas
Phone: + 242-394-2200
Fax: + 242-394-2244
Bottlenose Dolphins

The Dolphin Experience
PO Box F-43788
Freeport, Grand Bahama Island
Bahamas
Phone: + 242-373-1250
Fax: + 242-373-3948
E-mail: dolphexp@batelnet.bs
Web site: http://www.dolphinexperience.com
Bottlenose Dolphins

BELGIUM -

Boudewijn Park
Alfons De Baeckestraat 12
B-8200 Brugge
Belgium
Phone: + 50-38-38-38
Fax: + 50-38-23-43
Email: boudewijnpark@unicall.be
Bottlenose Dolphins, California Sea Lions, Harbor Seals

BERMUDA -

Dolphin Fantaseas - Bermuda
PO Box SN 698
Southampton, SNBX
Bermuda
Phone: + 441-238-4723
Fax: + 441-238-8331
E-mail: info@dolphinfantaseas.com
Web site: http://www.dolphinfantaseas.com
Bottlenose Dolphins

Dolphin Quest, Bermuda
c/o Southhampton Princess
PO Box HM 1379
Hamilton
Bermuda
Phone: + 239-6957
Fax: + 238-4176
E-mail: dqbermuda@ dolphinquest.org
Web site: http://www.dolphinquest.org
Bottlenose Dolphins

CANADA -

Dolphin Lagoon, West Edmonton Mall
#2472 8882-170 Street
Edmonton, Alberta
T5T 4M2
Canada
Phone: + 780-444-5333
Fax: + 780-444-5266
Web site: http://www.westedmall.com
Bottlenose Dolphins

Granby Zoo
525 St. Hubert Street
Granby, QC
J2G 5P3
Canada
Phone: + 450-372-9113
Fax: + 450-372-5531
Web site: http://www.zoogranby.qc.ca
Grey Seals, Harbor Seals

Marineland of Canada
7657 Protage Road
Niagara Falls, Ontario
L2E 6X8
Canada
Phone: + 905-356-8250
Fax: + 905-374-6652
Web site: http://www.marinelandcanada.com
Killer Whales, Beluga Whales, California Sea Lions, Harbor Seals

Toronto Zoo
361 A Old Finch Avenue
Scarborough, Ontario
M1B 5K7
Canada
Phone: + 416-392-5900
Fax: + 416-392-5966
South African Fur Seals, Polar Bears

Vancouver Aquarium
PO Box 3232
Vancouver, British Columbia
V6B 3XB
Canada
Phone: + 604-685-3364
Fax: + 604-631-2525
Web site: http://www.vanaqua.org
Beluga Whales, Pacific White-Sided Dolphins, Harbor Seals,
Stellar Sea Lions, Sea Otters

CUBA -

Aquaruio Nacional De Cuba
Primera Y. Avenue 60
Miramar, Playa C. Habana
Cuba
Phone: + 53-723-6402
Fax: + 53-724-1442
Bottlenose Dolphins

DENMARK -

Copenhagen Zoo
SDR Fasanveirj 79
DK-2000 Frederiksberg
Denmark
Phone: + 36-30-25-55
Fax: + 36-44-24-55
Harbor Seals, California Sea Lions

Fjord and Baelt Centre
Margrethes Plads 1
DK-5300 Kerteminde
Denmark
Phone: + 65-32-42-00
Fax: + 65-32-42-64
Web site: http://www.fjord-baelt.dk
Harbor Porpoises, Harbor Seals

DOMINICAN REPUBLIC -

Manati Park
Carretera Manati
S/n Bavaro/Higuey
Republica Dominicana
Phone: + 221-9444
Fax: + 221-9282
Bottlenose Dolphins, South American Sea Lions

ENGLAND -

Bristol Zoo Gardens
Clifton, Bristol BS8 3H
England
Phone: + 01-179-73-8951
Fax: + 01-179-73-6814
South American Fur Seal

Colchester Zoo
12 Guithavon Road
Witham Essex, CM8 1HD
England
Phone: + 01-206-33-1292
Fax: + 01-206-33-1392
E-mail: animals@colchester-zoo.co.uk
Harbor Seals, South American Sea Lions

Dolphin Services – Bloom UK
c/o Sea Lion Centre
Flamingo Land, Malton
North Yorkshire, Y017 6XW
England
Phone: + 01-653-66-8371
Fax: + 01-653-66-8541
Bottlenose Dolphins, South American Sea Lions, California Sea
Lions, South African Fur Seals

Woburn Wild Animal Kingdom
Woburn Park
Bedsford MK 17 9QN
England
Phone: + 01-525-29-0407
Fax: + 01-525-29-0489
California Sea Lions

FINLAND -

Dolphinariun Tampereen Sarkanniemi OY
Sarkanniemi, FIN-33230
Tampere
Finland
Phone: + 3-2488-111
Fax: + 3-2121-279
Web site: http://www.sarkanniemi.fi
Bottlenose Dolphins

FRANCE -

African Safari Zoo
41 Rue Des Landes 31830
Plaisance Du Touch
France
Phone: + 56-186-4503
Fax: + 56-106-7018
South American Sea Lions

Marineland Antibes
306 Avenue Mozart
06600 Antibes
France
Phone: + 61-116-5336
Fax: + 49-395-0209
Web site: http://www.informa.fr/Marineland
Killer Whales, Bottlenose Dolphins, Southern Sea lions, California
Sea Lions, Southern Elephant Seals, Harbor Seals, Grey Seals

Nausicaa
Centre National de la Mer
Boulevard Sainte-Beuve, BP 189
66203 Boulogne-sue-Mer
France
Phone: + 32-130-9999
Fax: + 32-130-9394
California Sea Lions

Parc Asterix
B.P. 8
Plailly 60128
France
Phone: + 3-44-62-3447
Fax: + 3-44-62-3456
Bottlenose Dolphins, Southern Sea Lions

Zoo De La Palmyre
B.P. 08
17570 Les Mathes
France
Phone: + 54-622-4606
Fax: + 54-623-6297
Email: zoopalmyre@eurodial-com.fr
California Sea Lions, Polar Bears

FRENCH POLYNESIA -

Dolphin Quest French Polynesia
c/o Moorea Beachcomber Parkroyal
B.P. 1021 Papetoai
Moorea 98729
Polynesia Francaise
Phone: + 689-56-38-76
Fax: + 689-56-16-67
E-mail: dqmoorea@ dolphinquest.org
Web site: http://www.dolphinquest.org
Bottlenose Dolphins, Rough-toothed Dolphins

GERMANY -

Delphinarium Muenster GmbH
Sentruper Strasse 319
D-48161 Muenster
Germany
Phone: + 251-81533
Fax: + 251-88721
Bottlenose Dolphins, California Sea Lions, Tucuxi Dolphin

Delphinarium Zoo Duisburg
Mulheimenstr, 273
47058 Duisburg
Germany
Phone: + 020-330-55961
Fax: + 020-330-55922
Bottlenose Dolphins, Beluga Whales, Amazon River Dolphins,
South American Fur Seals, California Sea Lions, Harbor Seals

Dortmund Zoological Garden
Mergelteichstraße 80
44225 Dortmund
Germany
Phone: + 231-502-8588
Fax: + 231-712-175
South American Fur Seals, California Sea Lions

Tiergarten Nurnberg
Am Tiergarten 30
D-90480 Nurnberg
Germany
E-mail: tg@stadt.nuernberg.de
Bottlenose Dolphins, California Sea Lions, West Indian Manatee

Tierpark Rheine
Eichenweg 1
48499 Salzbergen
Germany
Phone: + 49-59-715-5666
Fax: + 49-59-715-5564
Harbor Seals

HONG KONG -

Ocean Park
Wong Chuk Hang Road
Aberdeen
Hong Kong
Phone: + 852-2873-8888
Fax: + 852-2873-5584
Web site: http://www.oceanpark.com.hk
Bottlenose Dolphins, False Killer Whales, California Sea Lions,
Grey Seals, Stellar Sea Lions, South African Fur Seal

IRELAND -

Dublin Zoo
Phoenix Park
Dublin 8
Ireland
Phone: + 01-677-1425
Fax: + 01-677-1660
E-mail: info@dublinzoo.ie
Web site: http://www.dublinzoo.ie
California Sea Lions

ISRAEL -

Dolphin Reef Eilat
Southern Beach
PO Box 104
Eilat 88100
Israel
Phone: + 76-371-846
Fax: + 76-375-921
E-mail: reef@netvision.net.il
Web site: http://www.dolphinreef.co.il
Bottlenose Dolphins

ITALY -

Aquario de Genova
Area Porto Antico
Ponte Spinola
16126 Genova
Italy
Phone: + 010-2488-087
Fax: + 010-256-160
Bottlenose Dolphins, Harbor Seals

Delphinario Rimini
Via Dante 19
Rimini (RN) 47037
16126 Genova
Italy
Phone: + 0541-50298
Fax: + 0541-50362
Bottlenose Dolphins

Narvalo S.R.L.
Via Milano, 63
47838 Riccione (RN)
Italy
Phone: + 541-60-1712
Fax: + 541-60-6590
Bottlenose Dolphins

JAPAN -

Enoshima Aquarium Marineland
17-25 Katase-Kaigan, 2-Chome
Fujisawa, Kanagawa Pref 251-0035
Japan
Phone: + 466-22-8111
Fax: + 466-22-2642
E-mail: info@enoshima-aquarium.co.jp
Web site: http://www.enoshima-aquarium.co.jp
Bottlenose Dolphins, False Killer Whales, Pacific White-sided
Dolphins, Risso's Dolphins, California Sea Lions, Stellar Sea
Lions, Southern Sea Lions, South African Fur Seal, Northern Fur
Seals, Harbor Seals, Sea Otters

Izu-Mito Sea Paradise Aquarium
3-1 Nagahama Uchiura
Numazu Shizuoka 410-02
Japan
Phone: + 559-43-2331
Fax: + 559-43-2336
Killer Whales, Bottlenose Dolphins, False Killer Whales, Pacific
White-sided Dolphins, Risso's Dolphins, California Sea Lions,
Stellar Sea Lions, Southern Sea Lions, South African Fur Seal,
Northern Fur Seals, Walruses, Spotted Seals, Sea Otters

Kamagawa Sea World
1464-18 Higashicho
Kamagawa-City, Chiba-Pref. 296
Japan
Phone: + 470-92-2121
Fax: + 470-93-3084
Killer Whales, Bottlenose Dolphins, False Killer Whales, Pacific
White-sided Dolphins, Risso's Dolphins, California Sea Lions,
Stellar Sea Lions, Southern Sea Lions, South African Fur Seal,
Northern Fur Seals, Walruses, Spotted Seals, Sea Otters

Marine World umino-nakamichi
18-28 Saitozaki Higashi-ku
Fukuoka City 811-0321
Japan
Phone: + 92-603-0400
Fax: + 92-603-2261
Bottlenose Dolphins, Pacific White-sided Dolphins, Finless
Porpoise, California Sea Lions, Southern Sea Lions, Irrawaddy
River Dolphins

Minamichita Beachland Aquarium
428-1 Okuda, Minhama
Chita Aichi 470-32
Japan
Phone: + 0569-87-2000
Fax: + 0589-87-3776
Bottlenose Dolphins, False Killer Whales, Pacific White-sided
Dolphins, Risso's Dolphins, Stellar Sea Lions, Finless Porpoise,
Walruses, Southern Sea Lions, Harbor Seals, California Sea Lions,
Southern Elephant Seals, Sea Otters

Niigata City Aquarium
5932-445 Nisifunami
Niigata City, 951-8101
Japan
Phone: + 025-222-7500
Fax: + 025-223-2824
Bottlenose Dolphins, California Sea Lions, Stellar Sea Lions,
Southern Sea Lions, Baikal Seals, Spotted Seals, Sea Otters

Okinawa Marine Research Center
3425-2 Yamada Onna-Son
Kunibami-Gun
Okinawa 904-0416
Japan
Phone: + 98-965-5024
Fax: + 98-965-5064
Bottlenose Dolphins

Osaka Aquarium
1-1-10, Kaigandori
Minato-Ku, Osaka 552-0022
Japan
Phone: + 06-6576-5545
Fax: + 06-6576-5540
Pacific White-Sided Dolphins, California Sea Lions, Spotted
Seals, Sea Otters

Shimane Kaiyokan
1117-0 Kushirocho
Hamada-shi
Shimane 697-0004
Japan
Phone: + 855-28-3613
Fax: + 855-28-3620
Beluga Whales, California Sea Lions, Spotted Seals

Shimonoseki Marine Science Museum
Kaikyokan
Arca Port 6 - 1
Shimonoseki, Yamaguchi 750-0036
Japan
Phone: +81-832-28-1100
Fax: +81-832-28-1139
E-mail: info@kaikyokan.com
Web site: http://www.kaikyokan.com
Bottlenose Dolphins, Finless Porpoises, Commerson Dolphins
Californian Sea Lions, South American Sea Lions, Larga seals

Yomiuriland Marine Aquarium
13294 Yanokuchi Inagi-City
Tokoyo 206
Japan
Phone: + 044-966-1111
Fax: + 044-954-4678
Amazon Manatees, California Sea Lions, Sea Otters

MEXICO -

Atlantida Cancun
S.A. de C.V.
Blvd. Kukulcan KM. 25
Zona Hotelera, Cancun, Q.Roo
Mexico
Phone: + 98-81-30-00
Fax: + 98-81-30-03
Bottlenose Dolphins

Dolphin Adventure
BESTO S.A. de C.V.
Ave mastil loc 13c
Marina Vallarta
Puerto Vallarta Jalisco 48354
Mexico
Phone: + 322-12125
Bottlenose Dolphins

Dolphin Discovery
Centro Commercial Playa Langosta #10
Zona Hotelera,
Cancun, Q. Roo 77500
Mexico
Phone: + 52-98-49-42-39
Bottlenose Dolphins, California Sea Lions

Six Flags Mexico
Carretera Pichacho al Ajusto #1500
Col. Héroes de Padierna
Mexico City
Mexico, D.F. C.P. 14200
Phone: + 52-5-7-28-72-00
Fax: + 52-5-7-28-72-90
Web site: http://www.six-flags.com.mx
Bottlenose Dolphins, California Sea Lions

Via Delphi
S.A. de C.V.
Km. 282 Carr. Chetumal – Pto. Juarez
Interior Parque Xcaret
Riviera Maya, Q.Roo,
Mexico
Phone: + 987-14-120
Fax: + 987-14-123
Bottlenose Dolphins

NETHERLANDS -

Dolfinarium Harderwijk
Strandboulevard-Oost 1
3841 AB Harderwijk
Netherlands
Phone: + 31-341-467-467
Fax: + 31-341-425-888
E-mail: info@dolfinarium.nl
Web site: http://www.dolfinarium.nl
Bottlenose Dolphins, False Killer Whales, California Sea Lions,
Stellar Sea Lions, Grey Seals, Walruses, Harbor Seals

NEW ZEALAND -

Marineland of New Zealand
290 Marine Parade
PO Box 123
Napier,
New Zealand
Phone: + 6-834-4027
Fax: + 6-834-4037
Website: http://www.marineland.co.nz
Common Dolphins, California Sea Lions, Leopard Seals

PALAU -

Dolphins Pacific
PO Box 10044 Deep Banana Lane
Koror,
Palau 96941
Phone: + 680-488-8585
Fax: + 680-488-4562
Bottlenose Dolphins

PHILIPPINES -

Ocean Adventure
Camayan Wharf
West Ilanin Forest Area
Subic Bay Freeport Zone, 2222
Philippines
Phone: + 63-47-252-9000
Fax: + 63-47-252-5883
E-mail: info@oceanadventure.com.ph
Web site: http://www.oceanadventure.com.ph
False Killer Whales, Bottlenose Dolphins, South American Sea
Lions

PORTUGAL -

Jardim Zoological de Lisboa
Baia dos Golfinhos
Estrada De Benfica, 158 1549-004
Lisboa
Portugal
Phone: + 1-7232944
Fax: + 1-7232958
Bottlenose Dolphins, California Sea Lions

Zoomarine - Mundo Aquatico S.A.
Estarda Nacional 125, Km 65,
Guia - 8200-864 Albufeira
Portugal
Phone: + 351-289-506305
Fax: + 351-289-560309
Web site: http://www.zoomarine.com
Bottlenose Dolphins, Southern Sea lions, South African Fur Seals,
Grey Seals, Harbor Seals, Harp Seals, Ringed Seals

RUSSIA -

Dolphinarium "Opo"
45, Novorossiyskaya Street Anapa
Kpasnodar Region 353410
Russia
Phone: + 1-7232944
Fax: + 1-7232958
Bottlenose Dolphins, Northern Fur Seals

SINGAPORE -

Singapore Zoological Gardens
80 Mandai Lake Road
729826
Singapore
Phone: + 36-08527
Fax: + 36-52331
Web site: http://www.zoo.com.sg
California Sea Lions

Underwater World Singapore
80 Siloso Road Sentosa
098969
Singapore
Phone: + 2799222
Fax: + 2750036
Indo-Pacific Humpback Dolphins, Dugongs

SOUTH AFRICA -

Bayworld Complex
PO Box 13147
Humewood
Port Elizabeth, 6013
South Africa
Phone: + 41-586-1051
Bottlenose Dolphins, South African Fur Seals, Sub-Antarctic Fur
Seals, Southern Elephant Seals

SPAIN -

Marineland Catalunya
CTRA. Malgrat A. Palafolls
08389 Palafolls, Barcelona
Spain
Phone: + 93-765-4802
Fax: + 93-765-4412
Bottlenose Dolphins, California Sea Lions

Marineland Mallorca
Garcilaso De La Vega 9
Costa d'En Blanes
07184 Calvia-Mallorca
Spain
Phone: + 971-675-125
Fax: + 971-675-554
Bottlenose Dolphins, California Sea Lions, Southern Sea Lions,
Harbor Seals

Marineland Tenerife
Parque De La Reina Bloque LL33
Grond 38640 Tenerife
Spain
Phone: + 922-715-266
Fax: + 922-714-803
Bottlenose Dolphins

Mundomar
Sierra Helada, Rincon de Loix
03500 Benidorm
Spain
Phone: + 96-586-9101
Fax: + 96-586-8889
E-mail: Mundomar@mundomar.es
Web site: http://www.mundomar.es
Bottlenose Dolphins, California Sea Lions, Southern Sea Lions,
South African Fur Seals, Harbor Seals

Zoo De Barcelona S.A.
Parc de la Ciutadella s/n
08003 Barcelona
Spain
Phone: + 93-225-6780
Fax: + 93-221-3853
Bottlenose Dolphins, California Sea Lions

Zoo de la Casa de Campo/ Madrid Zoo
28011 Madrid
Spain
Phone: + 711-9954
Fax: + 711-8163
Bottlenose Dolphins, California Sea Lions, Southern Sea Lions,
Southern Elephant Seals, Harbor Seals

SWEDEN -

Kolmarden
Kolmarden's Djurpark AB
618 92 Kolmarden
Sweden
Phone: + 11-24-90-00
Fax: + 11-24-90-45
Bottlenose Dolphins, South African Fur Seals, Harbor Seals, Grey
Seals

UKRAINE -

Dolphinarium Yevpatoriya
Kharkowskaia 25-12
Sevastopol 335003
Ukraine
Phone: + 65-6961-157
Fax: + 65-6955-428
Bottlenose Dolphins

Karadag Dolphinarium
 (Karadag Natural Reserve of Ukranian –
 National Academy of Sciences)
24, Nauka Street, P.O.Kurortnoe
Feodosiya 98188, AR the Crimea
Ukraine
Phone/Fax: +380-6562-38161
E-mail: poza@dolphin.crimea.com
Web site: http://www.dolphin.crimea.com
Bottlenose Dolphins, Northern Fur Seals

Oceanarium Aquamarine
2 Kornilov emb.
Sevastopol 335040
Ukraine
Phone: + 0692-544-203
Fax: + 0692-553-350
Bottlenose Dolphins, Beluga Whales, Southern Sea Lions, Stellar
Sea Lions, Northern Fur Seals, Walruses, Baikal Seals

State Oceanarium of Ukraine
Mailbox 74
Sevastopol 335003
Ukraine
Phone: + 69-2555-243
Fax: + 69-2555-243
Bottlenose Dolphins, Beluga Whales, Stellar Sea Lions, Harbor
Seals

PROFESSIONAL ASSOCIATIONS

The following organizations offer a great deal of valuable information about the animals and zoological professions they represent. Most of them now have Web sites that are updated regularly.

In addition to representing and supporting working professionals, most of these associations offer membership opportunities for students and other people who are genuinely interested in the profession, but not necessarily employed in the field. Newsletters, conference proceedings, periodic journals, membership directories, Web sites and other resource materials provide valuable information and insights to members. Updates on new facilities, volunteer and internship opportunities, and job postings and requirements are especially helpful in career planning.

For those people truly interested in a marine mammal care and training career, a membership in the International Marine Animal Trainers Association (IMATA) is highly recommended. A visit to the IMATA Web site will provide information about this organization and its membership policies, opportunities and application procedures.

Another important organization representing the marine mammal care and training profession is the Alliance for Marine Mammal Parks and Aquariums (AMMPA). Unlike IMATA, individual memberships are not available in this organization. Zoological parks, aquariums and other marine mammal operations actually form the membership body. Representatives are selected by the member institutions and govern the organization. Much of the Alliance's work focuses on educating the public about marine mammals, the zoological institutions that care for them and best practices for protecting wild populations and their critical habitats. A visit to the Alliance Web site should not be missed.

The following organizations are listed in alphabetical order:

Alliance for Marine Mammal Parks and Aquariums (AMMPA)
103 Queen Street
Alexandria, VA 22314
USA
Web site: http://www.ammpa.org

American Association of Zoo Keepers, Inc. (AAZK)
Administrative Offices
635 SW Gage Blvd.
Topeka, KS 66606
USA
Phone: +913-272-5821
Fax: +913-273-1980

American Zoo and Aquarium Association (AZA)
Office of Membership Services
Oglebay Park
Wheeling, WV 26003-1698
USA
Phone: +304-242-2160
Fax: +304-242-2283
Web site: http://www.aza.org

European Association for Aquatic Mammals (EAAM)
Web site: http://www.eaam.org

International Association for Aquatic Animal Medicine (IAAAM)
Web site: http://www.iaaam.org

International Marine Animal Trainers Association (IMATA)
1200 S. Lake Shore Drive
Chicago, IL 60605
USA
Phone: +312-692-3193
Fax: +312-939-2216
E-mail: info@imata.org
Web site: http://www.imata.org

Society for Marine Mammalogy (SMM)
Web site: http://pegasus.cc.ucf.edu/~smm/strat.htm

The marine mammal display, research and education community is a valuable partner in the conservation of wild populations and their critical habitats. For example, every year thousands of sick, injured and stranded marine animals (such as these two Northern elephant seal pups) are rescued, rehabilitated and returned to the sea by oceanariums, aquariums and other member facilities.

US GOVERNMENT AGENCIES

Protecting marine mammals and their wild habitats is important work. Over the past 30 years, much progress has been made in this critical ecological endeavor, and more still needs to be done.

The marine mammal display, care and research community has always been an important participant in this cause. Educating the public about these animals and the importance of protecting the marine environment is a top priority. Much of what we know about marine mammal physiology, behavior, sensory abilities, reproduction, etc., was discovered by working with animals living in marine parks and aquariums.

Many people are surprised to learn that not all species of marine mammals are classified as endangered. In fact, the majority of marine mammal species displayed in modern zoological facilities are not endangered. Many people are equally surprised to learn that, within the United States, all marine mammals are federally protected whether they are endangered or not.

Marine mammals are protected by numerous federal and state laws, including the Marine Mammal Protection Act, the Endangered Species Act, the Lacey Act, the Fur Seal Act and the Animal Welfare Act. Marine mammals in the wild are monitored and protected by both the National Marine Fisheries Service and the US Fish and Wildlife Service. Marine mammals cannot be taken from US waters without a federal permit issued by one of these two agencies. These agencies also maintain written inventories and track all marine mammals housed in US facilities. Obtaining a permit to collect from the wild is a long and difficult process, fully reviewed by government scientists and agencies, and open to public review and comment. Due to successful husbandry and breeding programs, requests for collections from the wild are rare today.

In addition, all facilities within the United States that house and display marine mammals must be licensed and regularly inspected by the US Department of Agriculture. These facilities must meet strict federal regulations that are called for in the Animal Welfare Act and published in the Code of Federal Regulations. All marine mammals living in US facilities, whether they were born in the wild or not, are protected by these regulations.

The following is an alphabetical list of federal agencies that regulate and maintain jurisdiction over marine mammals and marine mammal zoological facilities in the United States.

Animal and Plant Health Inspection Service
Animal Care
US Department of Agriculture
Unit 84
4700 River Road
Riverdale, MD 20737
USA
Phone: +301-734-4980
Fax: +301-734-4978
Web site: http://www.aphis.usda.gov

Marine Mammal Commission
4340 East-West Highway, Room 905
Bethesda, MD 20814
USA
Phone: +301-504-0087
Fax: +301-504-0099

NOAA/ National Marine Fisheries Service
Office of Protected Resources (F/PR1
1315 East-West Highway
Silver Spring, MD 20910
USA
Phone: +301-713-2289
Fax: +301-713-0376
Web site: http://www.noaa.gov

US Fish and Wildlife Service
Department of Interior
1849 C Street, NW
Washington, DC 20240
USA
Phone: +202-208-6541
Web site: http://www.fws.gov

The agencies listed above represent only a small portion of governmental bodies charged with protecting the world's marine mammal populations and ecosystems. Outside the United States, marine mammals are protected by laws and regulations enacted by individual countries and by international treaties and agreements.

COLLEGES AND UNIVERSITIES

The value of a proper education has been emphasized throughout this book. It is one of the fundamental keys to a successful marine mammal career. Many facilities require that their care and training staff possess a minimum of a four-year degree in such subjects as biology, animal behavior, psychology or other related disciplines. Luckily, most accredited colleges and universities around the world offer these types of courses and degree programs. While a degree specifically focused on marine mammals is not usually a prerequisite for employment as a trainer, some students may wish to narrow their concentration.

The following colleges and universities are some of the educational institutions within the United States that offer advanced course work and degree programs in marine mammalogy. They are listed in alphabetical order.

California State University
Moss Landing Marine Lab
PO Box 450
Moss Landing, CA 95039
USA
Phone: +408-633-7261
Fax: +408-663-0805

College of the Atlantic
105 Eden St.
Bar Harbor, ME 04609
USA
Phone: +800-528-0025
Fax: +207-288-4126
E-mail: inquiry@ecology.coa.edu

San Diego State University
Cetacean Behavior Lab
San Diego, CA 92182
USA
Phone: +619-594-5200
Fax: +619-594-1332
Web site: http://www.sci.sdsu.edu

Texas A&M University at Galveston
Marine Mammal Research Program
4700 Avenue U, Bldg. 303
Galveston, TX 77553
USA
Phone: +409-740-4718
Fax: +409-740-4717
E-mail: mmrpinfo@mmrp.tamu.edu
Web site: http://www.tamug.tamu.edu/~mmrp

University of California, Santa Cruz
Institute of Marine Sciences
A315 Earth and Marine Sciences Bldg.
Santa Cruz, CA 95064
USA
Phone: +408-459-2464
Fax: +408-459-4882
Web site: http://natsci.ucsc.edu/ims

University of California, Santa Cruz
Long Marine Laboratory
100 Shaffer Road
Santa Cruz, CA 950640
USA
Phone: +408-459-2883
Fax: +408-459-3383
Web site: http://natsci.ucsc.edu/ims

University of Hawaii
The Hawaii Institute of Marine Biology
PO Box 1346
Kaneohe, HI 96744
USA
Phone: +808-236-7401
Fax: +808-236-7443
Web site: http://www.soest.hawaii.edu/himb

Quite a few marine mammal trainers began their careers with a two-year associate's degree from Moorpark College's Exotic Animal Training and Management (EATM) program. Moorpark College is the only accredited institution in the United States that offers this type of program, which includes hands-on experience with large and exotic animals and course work on marine mammals. Entrance requirements are rigid, annual enrollment is very limited and the course work is intense. Moorpark's EATM program has an excellent reputation and a very good job placement record for its graduates. Some Moorpark graduates also go on to other colleges and universities to complete their bachelor's, master's or doctorate degrees.

Moorpark College
Exotic Animal Training and Management Program
7075 Campus Road
Moorpark, CA 93021
USA
Phone: +805-378-1441
Fax: +805-378-1499
Web site: http://www.moorpark.cc.ca.us
California Sea Lions

More information about colleges and courses for this profession can be found starting on page 42.

SCUBA CERTIFICATION PROGRAMS

Scuba stands for self-contained underwater breathing apparatus. Scuba tanks and equipment allow divers to stay underwater for prolonged periods of time without having to come to the surface to breathe. To rent scuba equipment, refill tanks and use this equipment safely you must take specialized courses and hold a valid certification from an accredited organization.

Marine mammal trainers work in and around the water much of the time. Most marine mammal facilities require their training staff to be scuba certified as a condition of employment. For some trainers, scuba diving is a regular part of their daily activity. There are many different courses and levels of certification available. In most cases, a basic diver or open water certification will fulfill the requirement.

There are several organizations around the world that offer approved dive and safety courses and issue scuba certification cards. Two of the most widely known organizations are the Professional Association of Diving Instructors (PADI) and the National Association of Underwater Instructors (NAUI). PADI and NAUI certification courses are most often taught through local dive shops and resorts. Check your local phone directory for a location near you.

Some high schools and colleges offer scuba safety and certification courses through their Physical Education departments. The YMCA has offered excellent scuba programs for many years. They also maintain a very good Web site with answers to some of the most frequently asked questions about safe scuba diving and certification programs.

YMCA SCUBA Program
Web site: http://www.ymcascuba.org
FAQ page:
        http://www.ymcascuba.org/ymcascub/dive.html

Professional Association of Diving Instructors - PADI
Web site: http://www.padi.com

National Association of Underwater Instructors – NAUI
Web site: http://www.naui.com

Like humans, dolphins are warm-blooded, air-breathing mammals. Unlike humans, however, dolphins are *naturally* adapted to life in an aquatic environment. They do not need specialized equipment and training to spend more than a few minutes below the water's surface.

SUGGESTED READINGS

Over the years, a lot of books have been written about marine mammals. Many are great sources of information about the animals' natural history, behavior, anatomy, physiology, care, training, etc. Unfortunately, some books contain old or inaccurate information. Some seem to be based upon fantasy and speculation. Perhaps this is due to the fact that marine mammals live in a world that is so foreign to most of us. Most people do not have direct access to whales, dolphins, seals and otters, unlike more familiar animals, such as dogs, cats and horses. Marine mammals can certainly seem more mysterious than other, more common, domestic, farm and zoo animals. This mystery has undoubtedly sparked many myths, legends, exaggerations and speculations about dolphins, whales and other creatures of the sea.

As stated earlier, there are many excellent books available on marine mammals. The following list represents only a few personal favorites. Each provides accurate information and is thoroughly researched and well-written.

Many of the Web sites hosted by zoological institutions and professional associations offer their own recommended lists of credible books and resource materials. For more recommended readings, check out some of the Web sites listed throughout this book.

Don't Shoot The Dog: The New Art of Teaching and Training
By Karen Pryor

A great introduction to training and behavior. Available almost anywhere and very affordable. For everyone, teens through adult. This book is a very enlightening, entertaining and easy-to-understand introduction to training, positive reinforcement and operant conditioning. Pryor uses a lot of everyday examples to illustrate her points, as well as many references to her years of work with dolphins and other marine mammals at Sea Life Park in Hawaii. *Don't Shoot the Dog* is an accurate and up-to-date classic. Even though it was written for everyone, it is required reading for many professional marine mammal trainers around the world.

Animal Training: Successful Animal Management Through Positive Reinforcement
By Ken Ramirez

First published in 1999, this book has become a definitive guide to marine mammal training. Authored by Ken Ramirez, Director of Training and Husbandry at Chicago's Shedd Aquarium, this publication is a "must have" for any professional animal trainer, or anyone, who wants to really understand the art and science of animal training. This book has quickly become required reading at many marine mammal facilities around the world.

The Bottlenose Dolphin: Biology and Conservation
By John E. Reynolds, Randall S. Wells and Samantha D. Eide

Comprehensive enough for professionals and educators but written in a style that everyone can learn from and enjoy. For teens through adult. Authored by well-known marine mammal experts and scientists John E. Reynolds, Randall S. Wells and Samantha D. Eide, this book replaces many of the common myths associated with these animals with modern scientific facts.

Pinnipeds: Seals, Sea Lions, and Walruses
By Marianne Riedman

One of the best general reference books available on seals, sea lions and walruses today. For everyone, teens through adult. Pinnipeds don't get nearly the amount of attention and press that dolphins and other cetaceans do, but they are certainly fascinating animals in every respect. This book covers the subject very well and offers some great photos and illustrations.

Dolphin Societies: Discoveries and Puzzles
by Karen Pryor and Ken Norris

Entertaining and informative reading. A very valuable reference source on cetacean behavior and research. For everyone, teens through adult. This is another excellent book by Karen Pryor and Dr. Ken Norris, two of the great pioneers in the field of marine mammal care, training, research and education. *Dolphin Societies* is written by people who really know and understand cetaceans. Unlike some books that tend to obscure the true nature of dolphins with bias, fantasy and supposition, this book provides an accurate window into this fascinating world.

The CRC Handbook of Marine Mammal Medicine
Edited by Leslie Dierauf

This book is primarily written for serious marine mammal professionals and students. It is certainly one of the most valuable single reference books available on this subject. Each chapter is written by some of the most respected specialists within their fields of expertise.

BIBLIOGRAPHY

Andrews B. Marine mammal husbandry and training. *American Association of Zoological Parks and Aquariums Regional Proceedings.* 1986. 318-319.

Bain D, Samansky T. Analyzing changes in dolphin survival rates over time at Marine World Africa USA. *International Association for Aquatic Animal Medicine Proceedings.* 1995. 26:60-64.

Brisby W. The training of a good keeper. *American Association of Zoological Parks and Aquariums Regional Proceedings.* 1985. 157-159.

Coombs L, Foye K, Magaw M, Manulikow C, Pereyra A, and Samansky T. The challenges encountered when adapting to a single killer whale. *International Marine Animal Trainers Association Proceedings.* 1999.

DeMaster DP, Drevenak JK. Survivorship patterns in three species of captive cetaceans. *Marine Mammal Science.* 1988. 4(4):297-311.

Desmond T, Laule G. Husbandry training: A gateway to enhanced socialization. *International Marine Animal Trainers Association Proceedings.* 1987. 55-62.

Dierauf LA. *CRC Handbook of Marine Mammal Medicine: Health, Disease and Rehabilitation,* Dierauf LA, Ed.. CRC Press Inc., Boca Raton, FL. 1990

Fad S. The killer whale (*Orcinus orca*). *International Marine Animal Trainers Association Soundings.* 1996. 21 (2): 18-32.

Gage LJ, Trupkiewicz J, Samansky T. Hydrocephalus in an aged California sea lion. *International Association for Aquatic Animal Medicine Proceedings.* 1995. 26:9-10.

Gaskin DE. *The Ecology of Whales and Dolphins.* Heinemann Educational Books Ltd., London. 1982.

Geraci JR. Husbandry, in *Zoo and Wild Animal Medicine*, 2nd ed., Fowler ME., Ed.. W.B. Saunders Co., Philadelphia, PA. 1986. 757-760.

Geraci JR, Lounsbury VJ. *Marine Mammals Ashore: A Field Guide for Strandings.* Texas A&M Sea Grant Publications, Washington, Galveston, TX. 1993.

Geraci JR. Nutrition and nutritional disorders, in *Zoo and Wild Animal Medicine,* 2nd ed., Fowler ME., Ed.. W.B. Saunders Co., Philadelphia, PA. 1986. 760-764.

Glen TB. *The Dolphin and Whale Career Guide.* Omega, Chicago. 1997.

Hofman RJ. The marine mammal protection act - A first of its kind anywhere. *Oceanus.* 1989. 32(1): 21-25.

Hoyt, E. *Orca: The Whale Called Killer.* Camden House Publishing, Ontario. 1990.

International Union for Conservation of Nature and Natural Resources. 2001 *IUCN Red List of Threatened Animals.* IUCN, Gland Switzerland. 2001

King JE. *Seals of the World.* 2nd ed., Comstock Publishing Co., Ithaca, NY. 1983.

Krajniak EF. Opening a new marine mammal exhibit. *International Marine Animal Trainers Association Proceedings.* 1987. 63-66.

Minasian SM, Balcomb KC, Foster L. *The World's Whales.* Smithsonian Books, Washington, D.C.. 1984.

Murphy K. The Living Seas Pavilion. *International Marine Animal Trainers Association Proceedings.* 1984. 94-100.

Negrini S, Samansky T, and Chapple J. Environmental enrichment and tusk development in four Pacific walruses (*Odobenus rosmarus divergens*). *International Marine Animal Trainers Association Soundings.* 1998. 23 (3): 18-20.

Pryor K. *Don't Shoot the Dog.* Simon and Schuster, New York. 1984.

Ramirez K. *Animal Training: Successful Animal Management Through Positive Reinforcement.* Shedd Aquarium, Chicago. 1999.

Ridgway SH. *Dolphin Doctor.* Dolphin Science Press, San Diego, CA. 1995.

Ridgway SH. Homeostasis in the aquatic environment, in *Mammals of the Sea: Biology and Medicine.* Ridgway SH., Ed.. Charles C. Thomas Publishers, Springfield, IL. 1972. 590-747.

Riedman M. *The Pinnipeds: Seals, Sea Lions and Walruses.* University of California Press, Berkeley. 1990.

Samansky T, Sieswerda P. The recovery, care, and transport of orphaned walrus calves at St. Lawrence Island, Alaska. *International Association for Aquatic Animal Medicine Proceedings.* 1995. 26:33.

Samansky T, Gage L, Rutherford S, Allen S, Turley P, and Chapple J. Hand raising orphaned walrus calves at Marine World Africa USA. *European Association of Aquatic Mammals Proceedings.* 1996

Samansky T, Rutherford S, Gage L, Allen S, Turley P, Chapple J. Hand raising orphaned walrus calves at Marine World Africa USA - the first year. *International Association for Aquatic Animal Medicine Proceedings.* 1995. 26:34-35.

Samansky T, Allen S. Walrus Experience: Marine World's Newest Adventure. *International Marine Animal Trainers Association Proceedings.* 1995. 23:16.

Samansky T, Desmond T, Fish L. Developing a marine mammal husbandry department within a foreign culture - a case study. . *International Marine Animal Trainers Association Proceedings.* 1992. 20:32.

Seal US. How zoos and aquariums help to maintain biological diversity. *American Association of Zoological Parks and Aquariums Annual Proceedings.* 1986. 70-77.

Shane SH, Wells RS, Wursig B. Ecology, behavior and social organization of the bottlenose dolphin: a review. *Marine Mammal Science.* 1986. 2(1): 34-63.

Skaar D. Stretcher training for handling whales and dolphins. *International Marine Animal Trainers Association Proceedings.* 1987. 35-38.

Spotte S. *Sterilization of Marine Mammal Pool Waters - Theoretical and Health Considerations.* United States Department of Agriculture, Animal and Plant Health Inspection Service. Technical Bulletin No. 1797, 10-1991.

Stephens B. Conditioning behavior for husbandry purposes. *American Association of Zoological Parks and Aquariums Annual Proceedings.* 1986. 216-217.

Sweeney JC, Ridgway SH. Procedures for the clinical management of small cetaceans. *Journal of the American Veterinary Medical Association.* 1975. 16: 540-545.

Sweeney J, Samansky T. Elements of successful facility design: marine mammals, in *Conservation of Endangered Species in Captivity: An Interdisciplinary Approach,* Gibbons EF, Durrant B, and Demarest J, Eds.. *State University of New York Press,* New York. 1995. 465-477.

Sweeney JC, Samansky TS, Solangi MA. Course of therapy utilized in a California Sea Lion with blastomycosis. *International Association for Aquatic Animal Medicine Proceedings.* 1987.

Turley P. The iceman cometh: A technique for weaning sea lion pups. *International Marine Animal Trainers Association Soundings.* 1988. 13(1):8.

United States Department of Agriculture, Animal and Plant Health Inspection Service. *Animal Welfare Regulations,* 9 CFR Chapter 1, 1-1-1992.

Van der Toorn J. A biological approach to dolphinarium water purification. *International Marine Animal Trainers Association Proceedings.* 1987. 131-132.

Wells RS, Irvine AB, Scott MD. The social ecology of inshore Odontocetes, in *Cetacean Behavior,* Herman LM., Ed.. John Wiley and Sons, New York. 1980. 263-318.

Wells RS, Scott MD. Estimating bottlenose dolphin population parameters from individual identification and capture-release techniques. Report from the *International Whaling Commission.* (Special Issue 12) 1990. 407-415.

White JR, Francis-Floyd R. Nutritional management of marine mammals. *International Association for Aquatic Animal Medicine Proceedings.* 1988. 19: 5-15.

INDEX

Trainers from the Point Defiance Zoo and Aquarium conduct a training session with the institution's beluga whales. Feeding, training and directly interacting with the animals are just some of the important duties of a marine mammal trainer.

For more information about marine mammals and the people who care for and train them, visit…

DolphinTrainer.com

http://www.dolphintrainer.com

The Marine Mammal Information Website

Quick Order Form

For fastest service:
Visit our website at:
www.dolphintrainer.com

For mail orders:
DolphinTrainer.com
1370 Trancas St. # 402
Napa, CA   94558

Please send ☐ copies of *Starting Your Career as a Marine Mammal Trainer* ($16.95 / copy) to:

Name: _____

Address: _____

City: _____

State: _____ Zip: _____

Country: _____

Telephone: _____ - _____

Email address: _____

Shipping to USA or Canada   = $4.50
Shipping to all other countries = $9.50

For addresses within California add 7.75% sales tax

Payment: ☐ Check   ☐ Money Order
☐ Visa   ☐ MasterCard   ☐ AMEX   ☐ Discover

Card Number: _____

Name on Card:_____

Expiration Date: _____

CPBM 128046